PARTNERS *for* LIFE

PARTNERS *for* LIFE

Jane Bidder

IN ASSOCIATION WITH
CANINE PARTNERS

Illustrations by Nina Bondarenko

ORION

Copyright © Canine Partners 2002
Illustrations © Nina Bondarenko 2002

First published in Great Britain in 2002 by
Orion Books
An imprint of the Orion Publishing Group Ltd
Orion House, 5 Upper St Martin's Lane,
London WC2H 9EA

A CIP catalogue record for this book
is available from the British Library

ISBN: 0 75284 747 3

Typeset by Selwood Systems
Midsomer Norton

Printed in Great Britain by
Butler & Tanner Ltd
Frome and London

CONTENTS

As a fledgling journalist, I was often sent out on what my magazine editor called TOT stories (Triumphs Over Tragedies) when men, women and children survived terrible catastrophes but came out the other side. I dedicate this book to everyone who has gone through that trough of despair and lived, not only to tell the tale, but to recount it with a smile on their face. In particular, I would like to remember my courageous mother whose last piece of advice to me was: 'Stop worrying. The worst *will* happen one day. But somehow you'll find the strength to get through it.' I am also grateful for the support of my husband, children and mentor Betty Schwartz.

But finally, and perhaps most importantly, I dedicate this book to the amazing men and women in it. Throughout my years as a journalist for several national magazines and newspapers, I have interviewed countless TOTs. But none of them have affected me as deeply as these incredibly brave Partners for Life. Their examples are inspirations to us all.

Jane Bidder

INTRODUCTION

In 1990 Anne Conway and Liz Ormerod started fundraising to set up a charity to train assistance dogs who would be able to help people with disabilities in their daily lives. I was employed in 1992 to develop a programme to select and train puppies to become assistance dogs.

Those early days were fraught with difficulties: the organisation was financially insecure and lacked adequate training facilities. I was kept very busy finding and training puppies, selecting the right people for the dogs, keeping up with the administration and office work, as well as raising money, and giving demonstrations and presentations to tell the world about these special dogs. Originally the charity was called Assistance Dogs for Disabled; the final name, Canine Partners: Opening Doors to Independence, was agreed upon because we want to emphasise the partnership between dog and person, as well as the fact that these dogs open doors to independence for people with disabilities.

Today, Canine Partners dogs are famous all around the world, winning awards and acknowledgement for their talents and remarkable abilities. Representatives from similar dog-training programmes operating in other countries, especially the USA, visit Canine Partners to find out how we have been able to achieve such successful results. Our unique Puppy Education System is now being tried in other programmes, and I speak to conferences worldwide, explaining how Canine Partners brings out the best in puppies and develops their potential to become 'the hands and feet' for disabled people.

Assistance dogs need to be 'on call' when living with a person with disability. They must also be sensitive to the needs of that person, yet resilient and stable in any circumstances. Since we do not know the precise nature of the limitations or skills of a potential recipient, we train all our puppies to work at the highest level so that they can easily adapt to the specific requirements of any situation in which they are placed.

One of our partnerships, Allen Parton, has Canine Partner Endal. When Allen and Endal had successfully completed all the training, testing and assessment of the Residential Training course, they began to work together as a team. Endal was not a dog who responded willingly for most people, but because he worked readily for Allen, the dog showed that he had 'chosen' Allen as a suitable partner. This rapport was strengthened during the difficult and challenging training course, and further developed once they began encountering real-life situations. One day Endal observed Allen struggling to see the receipt and money at a cashpoint and reached up to help. Allen praised the dog and reinforced the behaviour, as he had been taught on the training course. Endal thereafter automatically participated in the transactions, and then learned to put the card in the slot! This talent won him Dog of the Millennium, Pro-Dog of the Year Gold Medal, and RSPCA Golden Bone Dog of the Year.

How is it possible for a dog to learn such complex skills and then continue developing in a similar way to that expected of children? Dogs that work at such a high level, and particularly with people with limited movement or mobility, must be highly motivated. They need to enjoy the work, and the work needs to be rewarding, because they cannot be coerced to do anything. And they will be asked to perform some very difficult tasks. For instance, they work off-lead inside the house, and may need to put on their own lead and collar and then take off their lead for free exercise in the park. They may be required to call the lift in a shopping centre or hospital.

Through their weekly training sessions of errorless learning and problem-solving, the puppies develop a positive attitude to any form of learning. They associate learning an activity with a powerful sense of achievement and excitement, so they are highly motivated to figure out ways to help their human handlers in daily activities.

The ideal assistance dog is one that not only observes the owner and the normal daily routine but also notices any signs of change in the owner's behaviour or ability and uses initiative to step in and help if needed in a particular situation. This is important because if the person's condition suddenly deteriorates or there is an emergency, there will be no time to train the dog to do something extra to assist. A dog that is in tune with the owner offers obedient responses as well as emotional support and rapport. Many of our dogs know immediately when a person is having a bad day and stay close by, keeping the person company. You can't make a dog do that!

When I began to train the first four Canine Partners in 1992, I had a fairly good idea of what dogs were capable of doing to assist people in their daily lives. What I didn't realise was just how much they were actually prepared to do. And how much they could teach me.

These dogs seem to work magic with their human partners. I am always moved when I see the incredible courage and determination of the people on the residential training course, their willingness to overcome all pain and difficulty in order to graduate with a Canine Partner. The dogs not only trigger changes in the person but also come up with ingenious and insightful ways to help their human partners. When I started this work I could never have foreseen that one dog would figure out to put the purse in the person's mouth when their hands became too weak to hold the purse. Or that another dog would place his half-chewed bone on his owner's lap, pick up and hand over a dropped phone without command, and then take back his bone. Or that a dog who hates having his feet touched would nevertheless hold his paws up to his partner for a splinter to be removed. Every person who has one of our dogs can tell you moving, funny, extraordinary or wonderful stories.

After ten years of training, I am still moved to tears by the people who triumph over difficulties for the sake of the dog, and by the dogs who choose to help, support, assist, comfort and encourage, and often just amuse and lighten the load. Despite having to confront the limits of their abilities and the reality of their condition on the residential training course, many students laugh more in those two weeks than they have for a very long time, simply because the dogs were delighting in being with them and sharing their lives.

Dogs are very zen – they live each moment to the maximum and this can be a very healing experience. It is remarkable to me that the dogs so consistently choose to work with their human partners. The dogs are free to go; the people have no means of forcing compliance or coercing obedience. The dogs have to want to help. Across the UK and Ireland, Canine Partners dogs are choosing to assist, choosing to nurture and choosing to take responsibility when necessary.

The remarkable stories in this book demonstrate how the dogs take their jobs very seriously but with endless good humour and joy of life. A Canine Partner is truly an incredible gift that can genuinely work wonders.

Nina Bondarenko
Programme Director
Canine Partners

FOREWORD

The bond between man and dog is one of life's wonders. More
so than any other animal, dogs have a hold on our hearts.
They love unconditionally, are unswervingly loyal, greet us
joyfully, keep us company and guard our property. They take
their place at the heart of the family, teach children responsibility, provide companionship for the lonely and are an
undemanding comfort to the unhappy. A cold and trusting
nose pushed into your hand and an adoring gaze meeting
yours are the best therapy. They also, it must be said, force
us out in the rain, bark senselessly at passing birds, dig up
our prize lettuces and leave a trail of mud and moult in their
wake. But they are, without doubt, worth it.

But for some people, dogs mean more still. For some, it is
the dog's special qualities – intelligence, sympathy and
devotion – which not only enhance life, but make it worth
living. Most of us are fortunate; we go about our lives taking
for granted our ability to go to work, visit friends, go on
holiday, drive, walk and simply enjoy our independence. But
for the less fortunate among us, even the most mundane –
but crucial – ingredients of an independent life such as
shopping, getting cash from the machine and calling a lift
become challenges. It is easy to see how people can become
isolated and their relationships with friends and family
strained. But the Canine Partners in these stories can – and
do – change all that. Not merely companions, but life supports
on four legs, constantly alert, they bring joy as well as assistance into the disabled person's life. Emptying the washing
machine, reaching a cereal packet from the cupboard, helping to remove a jacket or a pair of socks… it is hard to believe

what these dogs can achieve. Endal, for example, the extra-ordinary 'Dog of the Millennium' not only lifts the loo seat for his master – and fails to put it down again! – but he also wakes him up at 7 am, gets out his clothes for him and can even do up the zip on his jacket. Another finds lost keys and turns on light switches. Yet another brings a cardigan to his mistress, knowing instinctively when she is cold.

I have worked with Canine Partners since its early days and yet I never fail to be amazed at what the dogs and their partners can achieve. But the dogs are far more than just assistants – the bond between man and dog goes far deeper than that. They are friends and allies. The dogs love to help and there is an interdependence, an empathy and an under-lying affection that is hard to miss. Canine Partners is a truly worthwhile charity, and one I am proud to be involved in. It is impossible to read this book without being totally enthralled and entertained. It is a fitting tribute to a wonderful charity.

Penny Vincenzi

BADAR *and* DAVID

Badar, a beautiful golden retriever, sits up straight between the passenger and driver seat of the big converted Ford transit van, his eyes firmly focused on 55-year-old David Brown. Because of his rheumatoid arthritis, David is steering with an upright handle that is specially designed for people who have difficulty gripping a steering wheel. Badar is restless. He isn't particularly keen on travelling, not even short journeys. Despite this, he looks up at David trustingly, with large melting brown eyes. 'I don't like this one little bit,' he seems to say. 'But I'll go along with it. Anywhere you go, I go too.'

Canine Partners dogs like Badar have an incredible bond with their human partners. Indeed, Badar's close relationship with David goes beyond words. He knows what David wants to do almost before David does himself. He needs that wheelchair out of the back? No problem. Badar leaps out to steady the chair as David eases it out of the van. He needs that packet of cereal out of the cupboard at the back of the van? Fine. Badar will tug on the cord pull attached to the handle, gently pick up the packet with his teeth and bring it carefully over to David without dropping it once.

David is one of the few Canine Partners recipients who has been with the charity from its early days. But back in 1984, he'd never heard of Canine Partners or, indeed, assistance dogs. Until then, he'd been a happy-go-lucky bus driver who was known as being a steady, reliable employee. He enjoyed sports and was happily living with his partner Barbara. Then, one frosty spring morning, on his way to an early shift at 7 am, his life changed for ever. As he walked along the pavement, he slipped on a patch of ice and, to his annoyance, broke his elbow. Still, fractures like this can happen to anyone, he told himself. Within a few months, he'd be back to normal.

If only. The pain in his elbow worsened rapidly, spreading to the rest of his body. Hospital tests proved what he had begun to fear – rheumatoid arthritis had set in with a vengeance. Doctors told him that the illness had probably been initially triggered by the rheumatic fever he had in his twenties and then precipitated by the fall. David tried to go back to work but it was difficult; by now the rheumatoid arthritis was spreading. Nine months after the accident, he woke up to find his knees had locked. Terrified, he called out to Barbara, 'I can't move. Call an ambulance.'

David was rushed to hospital and given painkillers and physiotherapy. Although this helped David regain the use of his knees, it was difficult to get around without a walking frame or a wheelchair. Finally, he accepted the bitter truth: he would never be able to go back to work.

Imagine being able to run for the bus one month and, almost overnight, finding yourself unable to walk. It's the kind of tragedy that many of us can scarcely even envisage. Even worse, the repercussions of such disabilities also affect loved ones. For many years, David had been happily living with Barbara. Suddenly, the balance of their relationship had to change. David now needed help to do the simplest of tasks. Just as significantly, he was no longer able to bring home a wage. Unlike an accident, which might have brought in insurance money, David's illness merely entitled him to a disability payment, which took months to process.

But David was made of stern stuff. As difficult as it was, he accepted that the home he had built up with Barbara was now totally unsuitable with its spiral staircase. Reluctantly, they sold it to raise the £25,000 needed for a converted van that would take the electric wheelchair he now required. They moved into a rented ground-floor flat with wide doorways and other adapted features.

David tried to keep himself busy by setting up an information centre for disabled people in the community centre next to his new home in a small Hampshire village. He also got involved with local voluntary action groups to improve the lot of disabled people. Meanwhile, David's needs meant he required 24-hour care. Because they couldn't afford to hire carers, Barbara was forced to give up her job as a cook to look after David. But understandably, the stress and strain of such a responsibility took its toll, and Barbara began to feel physically and mentally weighed down. She also developed a dislike to going out of the house. 'We visited a counsellor to talk through the effects of my illness,' says David. 'She didn't provide any solutions but it helped us realise we weren't alone. Even so, it was very difficult.'

Something had to change. Then, by chance, David saw a television programme about a group of people who were trying to set up a charity to train dogs to help disabled people. This, however, was no ordinary charity. David had, of course, heard of guide dogs for the blind and hearing dogs for the deaf. But these dogs from a Dutch organisation, on the television in front of him, were doing some quite extraordinary things. They were opening doors, turning on light switches and picking up dropped objects. But it wasn't just the practical help they could offer; there was also an amazing bond between the dogs and their trainers and it shone out at David like a light from the terrible darkness that had surrounded him.

David already had a dog, Ellie, a schipperke, but the idea of a dog that was more than a pet was very appealing. He contacted the group (which was later to call itself Canine Partners) and offered his services as a fundraiser. It was a generous act because, at this early stage of the charity's progress, when it was still trying to raise enough money to get off the ground, there weren't any trained dogs available. At the back of his mind, David hoped that one day there might be an assistance dog for him. In the meantime, he was so impressed with the charity's aims that he was prepared to dedicate his free time to helping it work.

David and the other Canine Partners volunteers had some extremely hard work in front of them. Nowadays, when volunteers fundraise for the charity, they hold demonstrations to show what these amazing dogs can do. But in those days, there weren't any assistance dogs. Like the other early fundraisers, David had only a video showing what had been done by a similar group in Holland. It wasn't easy trying to persuade strangers to dig deep into their pockets for an unknown venture. But then David hit on the idea of taking Ellie with him. Although she wasn't an assistance dog, she was a real-life 'prop'. People would stop to stroke her and that gave David the opportunity to tell them what trained assistance dogs could do.

In order to spread the word, David visited local groups, schools and anyone who was interested. He also became a trustee for the charity, advising them on disability issues. It's easy to forget how tiring this kind of work can be for someone with severe rheumatoid arthritis. There were days when David would come back after a particularly exhausting fundraising event and collapse into bed. Some of us might have wondered if this incredible effort was worth it. After all, supposing the charity never got off the ground? But David never lost hope. If he could help others in his position, he would carry on until his last breath.

Then in 1992, came the breakthrough they had all been waiting for. Canine Partners had raised enough funds to buy and train three dogs! David could hardly believe it. It was the start of the charity's dream. If these dogs could drum up enough publicity, they would bring hope to thousands of disabled people who desperately needed another pair of hands, or paws, so that they could continue to be as independent as possible. Now it was up to Canine Partners and its loyal following to do what they could.

As a trustee, David was deeply involved. He was also extremely useful to the charity. Because of his condition, he was an ideal 'prop' for the trainers and dogs to practise on. So David's life changed once more. As well as continuing to fundraise, he also took part in training sessions, which enabled the dogs to get used to working with a wheelchair-user. For his part, David could hardly believe what these dogs could do. Although he loved Ellie deeply, she could follow only basic commands such as 'Heel' and 'Sit' and not always then! The assistance dogs, however, were a dream. All David had to do was utter a certain command, and they would bring in the phone, shut the door, pick up his crutches or bark for help. It was like having his very own four-legged genie.

David loved all the dogs but he had a soft spot for Alfred, a lovely golden retriever. (All the dogs in this first group had names beginning with *A* to distinguish them from later groups.) Alfred had a very kind nature. While practising on David, he seemed to understand David's needs and the way in which he found it difficult to pick things up or move across the room. David couldn't help hoping that he might be considered as a partner for one of the dogs. He could already see how incredibly useful they would be for him. It's difficult to understand fully how frustrating and difficult it is for a disabled person to go about everyday life, unless you are disabled yourself. Dressing and undressing himself, for example, took David nearly half an hour, even with Barbara's help. If he had a dog, it would make life easier for Barbara and also make David feel more independent. But David also knew that there were other people in just as

5

much need. Just because he had been a fundraiser, didn't mean he was entitled to one of these very special dogs.

Then, 18 months later, David was given the good news. Provided he stepped down as a trustee, he could go on the first two-week residential course to see if he would make a suitable partner. However, there were still no guarantees. The training course is not just a test to find out if a man or woman can get on with a particular dog. It's also a huge test to see if that person can cope in a strange environment without the support of family and friends. For David, who had become dependent on Barbara and his own familiar environment, it was a steep learning curve. 'Going somewhere new seemed quite daunting. I had to use a strange bathroom and get used to a different bed. When you have limitations like I have, these are difficult to get used to.'

But David was determined to cope; this was his long-awaited break. He also took heart from meeting the two other people on his course, Ian Free and Pauline Lishman, both of whom were wheelchair-users. Unlike the other two, however, David had already met all three dogs. But as David explains, 'Even so, there was no certainty that I would definitely be teamed up with one for life. We all had to try them out and see if we gelled.'

Alfred soon made it clear. He liked David and worked easily for him. But there was something that wasn't quite right. Alfred, as David soon realised, was what he called a 'trade union' dog. In other words, he followed his instructions to the letter but never did a jot more than he was required to do. And even though David liked Alfred, it was difficult to build up a close relationship with the dog. Alfred, too, showed that he enjoyed David's company because he kept following him around. But David was acutely aware that during the first two years of his life, Alfred had built up a very close relationship with his trainers and also his puppy-walker – a family who had 'fostered' Alfred by providing a home while he was being trained.

Now David had to build up a similarly close bond, but in

the space of two weeks instead of two years. It was a great but daunting challenge. On top of this, Alfred was only human! He didn't always do exactly what he was told. If, during exercises, David dropped something, Alfred didn't always pick it up as instructed. 'I had to use dog psychology. If you keep repeating the instructions, dogs get bored. So I would wheel my chair round and get Alfred to come in from a different angle. Then he'd see the object in a new light and, hopefully, pick it up.'

The first week was challenging, but by the second week, David found it all began to come together. Alfred and David passed their final shopping test in Chichester where, among other tasks, they had to negotiate lifts, have a snack at an outside café with Alfred sitting quietly under the table, and use pelican crossings. Only then, were they able to go home together and start their new life.

This period, says David, was the start of the second stage of his life. Until then, it had been a constant struggle to cope with daily tasks and this agonising rheumatoid arthritis. Alfred was the answer he had been waiting for. He was everything – and more – that David could have hoped for. And the difference he made to his life was extraordinary. 'It was as if a huge burden had been taken off both me and Barbara,' says David. 'Suddenly I had someone who could pull off my shoes and the rest of my clothes, item by item. I had another pair of "hands" and "feet" to help instead of having to rely on my partner. Although Barbara didn't mind helping, I did. Having Alfred gave me back some of my self-respect.'

That wasn't all. Alfred became his daily 'help' around the house. He could open cupboards and accompany David to his local shop. When David couldn't reach a cereal packet on the top shelf, he would give the command and Alfred would stand on his back legs and carefully bring it down. At the checkout, he would even hand over David's wallet to the cashier. Other shoppers couldn't believe what they were seeing. What kind of dog was this? So David told them in the hope they would spread the word. In this way, having his own dog not only saved David but also helped to get Canine Partners the publicity and credibility it so deserved.

Alfred also brought joy to Barbara's life. She loved him as a pet and for the help he provided in caring for David. Even Ellie seemed to get on well with Alfred, mainly because she could boss him around! For the first time in several years, the couple was able to forge some kind of normality.

But their hopes were short-lived. David's rheumatoid arthritis worsened and he found himself increasingly reliant on his chair. He also had to go into hospital for periods up to two or three months for knee operations. At that time, dogs were not allowed to visit the hospital, and to David's disappointment, he found that each time he came out, Alfred was less responsive to his commands. 'He would do what I said but it took longer and he was very bouncy and over-lively.'

Tragically, the bond between them was breaking down, because of David's enforced hospital stays. One factor underlying the successful partnership between assistance dogs and their partners is that the two rarely let each other out of their sight. Their exclusive relationship depends on their proximity and reliance on each other. An assistance dog thrives on praise for doing something right. But if its partner isn't there to do this or give commands, the dog becomes unsure of its role. After all, Alfred had been trained to follow commands; it was as if the dog had lost his job. With David away from the home, their special relationship was weakening. For David, ill in hospital, it was one more burden to bear.

Difficult as it was, Nina Bondarenko, Canine Partners' programme director, decided something had to be done. Alfred had been with David for only two years but it was time for him to go back for more training, to reinforce the lessons he had learned as a puppy but forgotten during David's absences. But where did that leave David?

It so happened that 18 months earlier, Nina had been approached by a breeder who wanted to sell one of her golden retriever puppies to the charity. They weren't cheap: the charity has to buy them at the going rate, which can be between £300 and £600 each. Nina picked two from the litter; one, she called Badar, and the other Biggles. Badar was lively but very intelligent. He was also highly competitive. At puppy class he would vie with Bridie (who later became Caroline Jarman's dog) and they would outstare each other over a toy they both wanted. Badar invariably won. But at the same time, he was also a softie who loved affection. He, too, had his own health problems, having been diagnosed as mildly dysplastic as a puppy. The best treatment was a con-centrated walking programme to strengthen his muscles. This would be difficult for some wheelchair-users but David felt he had the time to give to Badar's walking programme.

Even so, it was very difficult for David to transfer his affections from Alfred to another dog. When David took Badar home, it was like bringing back a stranger. 'We had to get to know each other and gain each other's confidence. The first day was awful. I kept thinking "Alfred would have done that differently" so I made myself blank Alfred out of my mind.' Instead, David threw himself into playing with Badar and finding out which toys he liked best. He soon found that he had to be much more sensitive to Badar's slightly 'soppy' nature. Alfred hadn't minded if David had raised his voice in disapproval, but Badar was easily upset and would retreat miserably to his basket. David learned that Badar shone when he was praised; so, in line with the Nina's errorless puppy training during which good behaviour was rewarded with treats and the wrong behaviour was ignored, David began to concentrate on telling Badar when he had done the right thing.

Meanwhile, they still had to 'graduate' formally before they could be officially partnered. The charity had never had to replace a dog before so, unlike present practice where partners still have to go through a training course, David and Badar took their tests in Chichester without having had any further training. In fact, the only mistakes came from David.

'When I'd taken the test with Alfred a few years earlier, the shops had been laid out differently. I was a bit thrown when I took Badar into the menswear department of Marks & Spencer and found it was now full of ladies' lingerie. But Badar didn't seem to mind. The height of the reception desk at the building society was also different. Badar had never been outside that particular café before and to get him to sit under the table, I had to quietly feed him treats.'

After graduation, David slowly continued to cement a relationship with his new dog. It was a gradual process over the next six months without any blinding flashes of sudden love; it was more like a comfortable marriage without any passionate roller-coaster ups and downs. Amazingly, Ellie also accepted her new partner with ease.

Gradually, David, Barbara and their dogs were able to resume their new lives together. As secretary of the caravan section of the Disabled Drivers' Motor Club, David and Barbara often go to meetings, shows and weekends away, all over the country. Although Badar dislikes the travelling, he can't wait to jump down and explore the new caravan site. He loves discovering new places but his cautious streak never lets him do anything too daring. Yes, he loves paddling in the lake but he'll never go out of his depth. Badar also loves suppertime when David and Barbara fry bacon on the cooker in the back of their van. There's nothing like fresh air for making a dog feel peckish. And afterwards, there's often a game of bingo with the other holidaymakers and their dogs. David is the bingo caller with Badar lying by his chair.

Back at home, David runs the support group for Canine Partners members. His experience helps him advise people who are still getting used to their new four-legged assistants. 'New dogs sometimes try to push the boundaries,' he explains. 'If a dog won't immediately do something, it can help to go back to basic control commands like "Sit down" or "Stay" and then progress to what you want it to do. I might also advise someone to vary the walking route and take a left instead of a right turn so the dog doesn't get too complacent about what it's doing but is alert to new instructions.'

A successful dog and owner partnership, like a successful marriage, must be based on considerations for the other's needs. David used to take Badar with him when he helped in the local charity shop run by disabled people. But Badar got easily bored if he didn't have enough to do and began walking around as though to say 'Can't we go home now?' David now leaves Badar behind; it's only for a couple of hours and it means David can give Badar all his attention when he comes back.

David still goes to hospital every now and then for treatment. Not long ago, he was an in-patient for two months. But hospital rules have relaxed since Alfred's day, and Barbara was allowed to bring Badar in during visiting time. 'He seemed to understand that I couldn't go back with him when it was time to go,' says David, gently stroking the ruff of Badar's neck. 'When I have bad days at home and can't get out of bed, he is used to Barbara taking him for a walk. So he accepted that she looked after him when I was in hospital.'

Badar, too, needs as much care and attention as his master. This craving for love has given David something to think about, apart from his own needs. So although it was hard when Alfred had to go, it has all turned out for the best. Ironically, David and Badar recently bumped into Alfred at a museum in Hampshire. It could have been awkward but it was actually the best thing that could have happened. 'Alfred seemed to greet me enthusiastically with big licks but then turned his attention to something else. Badar, on the other hand, was continually looking up at me to see if I was all right. After the initial pang at seeing Alfred, I was incredibly grateful that I now had Badar. Maybe I had to see Alfred again to realise how much Badar and I meant to each other.'

As David looks back, he can hardly believe how far both he and Canine Partners have come since those early fundraising years at the start of the 1990s. From one small video, there are now sixty assistance dogs helping disabled men and women at every level of their everyday lives. To do this, the Canine Partners has had to rely on stalwarts such as David. Despite campaigning, it still doesn't receive any funding from the government and relies entirely on donations. Meanwhile, David himself will be grateful to the Canine Partners for as long as he lives. 'If I hadn't watched that television programme, I might never have heard of it. Canine Partners has changed my life. And I'll never stop trying to change it for others too.'

ENDAL *and* ALLEN

The Japanese television crew watched, cameras whirling, as Endal, the yellow Labrador leapt up at the cash machine and, with his mouth, 'handed' the credit card and a wad of ten-pound notes to his master, 42-year-old Allen Parton. 'That's amazing,' said producer Masaki Mochizuki from Super Television, one of Japan's national television networks. 'What else can he do?'

Endal was keen to show him. Back at Allen's home in Clanfield, Hampshire, he opened the washing machine with his nose, pulled out several pairs of socks, carefully dropping them into the laundry basket ready to hang on the line. Then, on command, he opened a kitchen cupboard, tugging at a purple cord hanging from the handle, and nosed out a packet of cereal, carrying it in his mouth to Allen in his wheelchair. Finally, he sat on the chair at the kitchen table, while Allen had breakfast, ready to 'hand' him anything he needed.

Four years earlier, however, when Endal was born, no one thought that this lonely little puppy was particularly special. If anything, he was something of a misfit since his parents, who were owned by a Southampton breeder, were father and daughter. Not realising that the bitch was still in season, the breeder had put her in with her father only to discover soon afterwards that she was pregnant. Such pregnancies can fail to develop or result in sickly or ill-formed pups. Amazingly, Endal, the only puppy in the litter, seemed perfectly normal. Even so, his owners, Barry and Sue Edwards, did not know what to do with him. Unable to register him because of his parentage, they considered keeping him as a pet until a month later when Canine Partners visited to inspect another litter.

'I happened to walk into the room and saw this very pretty puppy sitting all on his own,' recalls Nina Bondarenko, programme director for Canine Partners. 'I said, "Hello little yellow chap, what's the matter with you?" Then I asked if I could put him through the aptitude tests that we set dogs, to see if they would be suitable assistants for people who need help.'

These tests are a series of simple exercises to measure each dog's interest in people, co-operation, and flexibility. Nina started by placing Endal on his back to see if he licked rather than struggled. He did the former, which was a sign that he was adaptable and calm. Nina also put Endal in another room, which he didn't know very well, while she hid. The puppy sat and thought for a while and then started to search for her. This was exactly what Nina had been hoping he would do because it suggested he had initiative and wanted to be with people. Nina also gave him a spoon and then called him to her. Instead of hanging on to the spoon, he handed it over – another good sign. On the other hand, he wasn't very enthusiastic. He did some of these things rather half-heartedly as if he were saying 'Well I'll do it if you want but it is a bit of a bore.' Nina could also tell that he was sensitive and not the bravest dog in the universe; when she held him in the air, his body went rigid and he tucked his tail under. Nina's instinct (which she has learned to rely on during her thirty years' experience) told her that even if Endal wasn't as keen as she hoped, he would be right one day for someone.

So Canine Partners bought him from the breeder Barry Edwards and found Judith Turner, a 52-year-old dog-owner, to act as his puppy parent or 'foster mother'. Judith's job was to provide the stability and warmth of a family home and, at the same time, take him to puppy classes once a week. She also continued to practise these exercises, such as retrieving keys and shutting doors, outside class.

Judith had recently lost her 12-year-old black Labrador, Fennel, to cancer; when Canine Partners rang her up, she felt ready to take on a new challenge. What she quickly realised was that Endal, whom Canine Partners had named after a local vet, was a one-woman dog. Although he remained aloof during training sessions at the centre, he absolutely adored Judith and would lick her all over every time he saw her – even if she'd only walked out of the room for a few seconds. Judith lost count of the number of earrings she lost as a result of Endal's enthusiastic licks, which sent them flying across the room. 'He kept me on the straight and narrow after Fennel's death and would do absolutely anything for me. However, there was one big problem. Endal hated being alone at night and would get upset when we left him in his basket downstairs. Then, by chance, we thought of leaving a nightlight on. From that night on, he slept like a baby – he'd simply been scared of the dark. We also bought him a huge pink teddy bear to cuddle up to.'

Endal quickly became adept at jobs such as finding keys and taking off Judith's jacket. But his sensitive and loving personality also shone through when he was off-duty. 'He would play with the swallows in the field outside,' recalls

15

Judith. 'I've never seen anything like it. They would swoop down low and he would lift up his head to them just like a Disney cartoon. When I took him to a local village concert, he tried to outsing the chief tenor by howling above him. He also adored the smell of port. At Christmas, we came down-stairs to find he had opened a bottle of port with his teeth but left it standing upright on the carpet, without having spilt one drop. He had just wanted to sniff it one more time.

Yet as Endal continued to do his training at the centre with his former half-hearted attitude, Nina couldn't help thinking there was something missing. Somehow, despite his obvious intelligence, the dog lacked dynamism and didn't seem to sparkle. It was as though he were waiting for something or someone to happen in life in order to release his full potential. Endal was also the kind of puppy who was choosy about who he bonded with. When, as part of his training, he did a three-week swap with another family to help him adapt to different environments, Endal took a while to adjust. Although he did what he was told, he also closed down and withdrew into himself. Nina began to realise that she needed to find him a full-time partner whom he could really relate to, just as he had bonded with Judith. If she couldn't find the right person, Endal would never find his potential, and for an intelligent dog, that seemed a great waste.

There was another added complication. Endal was show-ing signs of going lame. 'Puppies often do this, on and off, as part of their growing process while their bones knit together,' explained Nina. 'It's known as panosteitis, like growing pains in children. But it was happening too often to Endal so we had him X-rayed. The results showed that he might have osteochondritis dessicans, a fault in the elbow joint. Some dogs get better on their own accord but others get worse and have to be operated on, which would mean they wouldn't be able to work. We weren't sure with Endal. He seemed too good a dog to waste, but at the same time, his future was seriously in doubt. So we decided to rest him and see what happened.'

Meanwhile, only five miles away, the future was looking even more bleak for 42-year-old Allen Parton. In 1991, Allen, then a weapons electronics officer in the Royal Navy, had waved goodbye to his wife, Sandra, and their two children, Liam and Zoe, age six and five, to fight in the Gulf War. As they set off, Allen and his men had been told that 15 per cent of them wouldn't come back. But like many brave servicemen, he was certain he would return. After all, he'd already served in the Falklands and Northern Ireland and come out unscathed. Why should his luck run out this time?

But it did. Within a month of arriving, Allen's military car was smashed up in a serious accident, which shattered both his body and mind for ever. His first memory was waking up in a British hospital six weeks later and thinking, 'Where am I?' His right-hand side had lost all feeling and he had lost fifty per cent of his memory. The effects were catastrophic. Allen couldn't recognise family or friends, let alone remember the names for everyday items such as a bed. He only knew Sandra was his wife because the nurses would say 'Your wife is here'. Even more terrifying, he couldn't recall getting married or having the children. In a flash – literally – Allen had gone from a healthy father of two to an angry, wheelchair-bound invalid who couldn't talk properly and whose words spilled out of his mouth in a haphazard, disorderly fashion without making sense.

'The fear and shock made me furious,' admits Allen. 'I refused to accept I was disabled and I'm ashamed to say that I was horrible and rude to everyone.' He was also plunged into a deep, fathomless depression from which there seemed no escape. Twice, he tried to commit suicide. It was, he told himself, the only way out.

Allen spent the next five years in hospital and rehabilitation. When he finally came home, Sandra, who had had to give up her job as a nurse to look after her husband, was at her wits' end. Then she saw an article about Canine Partners in a local newspaper. Desperate to do something for herself, as well as looking after Allen, she became a puppy parent to

Ferdy, a yellow Labrador. The distraction and light-relief provided by a lively puppy in the house, helped the whole family – even though Allen still found it difficult to talk and communicate.

One day, in the summer of 1997, Allen's usual bus for his day centre failed to turn up. Sandra told him, in no uncertain terms, that she wasn't prepared to have him moping around the house. He would have to go to the Canine Partners centre with her. Although he didn't see it then, Fate had just stepped in. Allen's life was about to change almost as dramatically as it had been changed by his accident. But as he sat in the training centre that morning, his wheelchair parked in the corner of the room, refusing to speak or join in, Allen didn't realise this. Instead, he would rebuff anyone who tried to ask him a question, by telling them to talk to his wife. He felt horribly self-conscious and uncomfortable and it was easy to see why. He was unable to speak clearly and his body was continually twitching. He refused to make eye contact with anyone.

Not far away from his chair sat a group of puppies, resting between training sessions. One of them happened to be Endal. 'He started looking at Allen and as he did so, Allen glanced back,' said Nina, who is constantly observing dogs and thinking about the applicants to see if they might fit. 'Endal then looked up again and seemed to say "Mmm, I quite like you" and then Allen put his hand down to give him a pat. Immediately, Endal leapt upon Allen's lap and gave a big slobbery grin. Allen smiled as though to say, "This dog really likes me!" Then, almost without knowing why he was doing it, Allen began to rub Endal under his red working jacket. It so happens that Endal *loves* being rubbed at exactly that spot. He looked up at Allen as if to say "You are my man!"'

It was nothing short of a miracle – a dramatic turning point that both Allen and Endal had needed so badly in their lives. And it sent, says Nina, a tingle down her spine. As Allen left the centre that day, there was a certain sparkle in his eyes, which hadn't been there for a very long time. He could hardly wait until the next week when Endal was coming back to the centre with his puppy parent. Allen made sure that he was there too, and over the next few weeks Endal made a beeline for him as soon as he came in through the door. The two would sit next to each other and Endal would reach out and touch him with his paw. As Nina points out, until he met Allen, Endal hadn't been anything special. It was the combination of his character with Allen's that made the winning ticket.

Just as Endal had helped Judith through her bereavement, it now seemed he wanted to help Allen. Even so, it wouldn't have been right for Nina to suggest that Allen and Endal be partnered immediately. She had to wait until Allen applied for a dog himself.

It took nearly five months for the assessment procedures and paperwork to go through. 'I had to fill in a form, describing my disabilities and this was the first time I had admitted there was something wrong with me,' recalls Allen. 'It was a cathartic experience, which finally gave me the hope I needed. Until I met Endal, I was in the depths of despair. But when he refused to leave my side in that training centre, I suddenly saw a chink of light. Endal had found me and wasn't going to let me go. He was living proof that angels don't just come on two legs.'

But before Allen could take Endal home, he had to go through an intensive twelve-day residential training course. During that time, Nina noticed a dramatic change in Endal's behaviour. 'Instead of doing jobs half-heartedly, he'd leap to it! Keys, he'd say, you want me to get keys? Great. Hang on and I'll run and get them. Before, when someone else was asking him to do it, he'd amble over to the keys and back again without any great incentive. In addition to his new enthusiasm, he seemed to have an understanding of how much Allen had been through. He's an interesting combination of pushiness and sensitivity.'

Endal's most amazing skill is his ability to use his initiative

19

and read situations quickly. This was exactly what Allen needed to help him cope with his severe injuries. Would Endal be able to help? They would soon find out when he joined the Parton household full-time in autumn 1997. Still unable to speak properly, Allen also suffered from word blindness when he simply couldn't find the words to give Endal a command. 'One morning, I realised I'd left my razor upstairs. I could see a picture of the razor in my head but couldn't think of the word. So I just patted my cheeks in an attempt to understand. To my amazement, he ran up the stairs and came down with it in its leather case.'

Over the ensuing months, Allen and Endal began to create their own sign language. A pat on the head means that Allen wants his cap. Instantly, Endal darts round to the back of the wheelchair where the cap is inside Allen's bag. Hands held up mean gloves are required, and Endal finds them and brings them round the front to Allen.

Allen and Endal began to be photographed by local newspapers, and then, as they grew in confidence, they were nominated for an award in a national competition run by *Dogs Today* magazine. During one photographic session, Endal and Allen went shopping at the local supermarket to show how Endal could differentiate between 'tins' and 'bottles' and nose out whatever Allen asks for on the shelves, such as a loaf of bread. As they were leaving, Allen realised he needed money from the cash machine outside. With the sunlight shining on the glass screen, making it difficult for Allen to see, and with the money and receipt slot set far up the back of the machine, Allen was struggling. Suddenly, without being asked, Endal jumped up to retrieve the card and money when Allen had made his transaction.

Newspaper photographs asked him to do it again and again so they could get their pictures. This was the photograph that was used when Endal was voted Dog of the Millennium in the *Dogs Today* competition. The result was a picture of Endal splashed over nearly every front page. The press went wild and reporters from around the world wanted to know about this extraordinary dog. He was filmed by crews almost daily. People started to recognise the yellow Labrador as 'Endal the Cashpoint Dog'.

But the most amazing example of Endal's initiative happened in May 2001 when the pair were invited to a stand at Crufts. After checking into the hotel the night before, Allen took Endal outside for a run across a green on the other side of the hotel car park. As usual his lead was clipped to the chair. Suddenly a car reversed towards them at 40 mph. Endal was between Allen and the car so, instinctively, Allen pushed the dog out of the way. Seconds later, the car knocked the chair over and Allen blacked out. When he came round, he found Endal pulling his body over, using his teeth on his jacket, to put Allen into the recovery position. The dog then ran back for his mobile phone, which he got out of the bag, and thrust against Allen's face. After that, he went back for his blanket from the chair and then ran up to the hotel reception, barking for help.

The story hit the national headlines. Endal, it appeared, was the first dog who had ever put a human into the recovery position, without being taught. Once again he was a familiar face on the television and in the news. Everyone wanted footage of this remarkable dog. But fame came at a price. Endal had overstretched himself by jumping up at the cashpoint so many times, and the following day, he went severely lame during a fundraising event.

Allen's world was crashing down around him once again. A lame dog would be unable to fulfill his work properly and could even be taken off the Canine Partners programme to be re-homed as a pet. Allen and Endal were in severe danger of losing each other unless they could do something about it. Determined to do something, Allen and Sandra visited several vets, all of whom agreed that strict rest was needed. However, this was difficult as Endal refused to leave Allen's side. When he left the room, so did the dog. Going upstairs exacerbated the lameness; Allen had always refused a stair-lift, preferring to be independent and get up and down on his bottom. So the only option was to shut Endal in the kitchen at night in an attempt to make him rest.

In the morning, however, the Partons found that Endal had jumped up and down the kitchen work surface and eaten a kilogram of rabbit food from its bag. 'It was as though he was doing it to attract attention and say "How dare you shut me out?"' said Allen. He also had the swing-bin lid round his neck, which could have been dangerous. There was only one solution to ensure strict bed rest: the kennels. Allen, in floods of tears, was unable to take Endal himself, so Alison, one of the Canine Partners trainers, volunteered.

For two weeks, Endal had to stay in a very small cage, which limited his movement. He had one short break and that was to the vet. Meanwhile, Allen admitted that he was acting like a bear with a sore head. 'I was angry with everyone and behaving like a child. By the end of two weeks, Endal was still limping. The vet said that he might get better but he might not.'

Endal came back home but Allen confessed that he was unable to cope with the uncertainty. 'If he came home and then had to go again, because of his health problems, it would have destroyed me. So Heather, the Canine Partners training manager, took Endal to her home for the night and put him back in kennels the following morning.'

No one, however, had reckoned on Endal's determination – or Sandra's. Furious with her husband, this feisty 42-year-old ex-nurse told him to stop being so selfish and to think of someone else instead of himself – that someone, of course, was Endal. She told Allen, in no uncertain words, that the dog needed him badly at this moment in his life but that Allen wasn't there for him. It was the best thing she could have said. Allen leapt into action. Unable to drive himself, because of his disability, he asked Alison to collect Endal from the kennels and bring him home, where he belonged. Even if Endal ended up limping for the rest of his life, Allen pledged to himself that he would be there to take away the dog's hurt and pain, just as Endal would do for him.

Endal came home, his tail wagging energetically with excitement. He and Allen were now a 'marriage' for better or for worse. During the next few months, Endal was put on a strict diet of additive-free meat and cereal to help his arthritis, along with a gentle exercise regime and a quiet period to heal. Slowly, he has continued to improve and, although Endal, like Allen, has bad days, the arthritis appears to be under control.

Meanwhile, miraculously, Allen's speech was improving dramatically and his twitching had almost stopped. Indeed, to hear him now, it's hard to believe that he was almost incomprehensible, despite five years of speech therapy. Neither Allen nor Sandra are certain how Endal achieved this, although Allen thinks it was because he desperately wanted to talk back to a dog who obviously loved him so much. Even more touching, Endal talks too. A dog normally uses about eight different voice patterns, but Endal has twenty. According to tone, they mean all kinds of things, ranging from 'I love you' to 'Can't we switch television channels?'. (His favourite programmes involve anything with animals in it.)

Allen lifts Endal onto his knee to tickle his huge tummy and demonstrate how he 'talks'. Endal looks up at his master adoringly and howls with pleasure. The noise is so loud that I half expect someone to knock on Allen's front door to see what's going on. In fact, the neighbours are used to it. Allen and his dog are well known in Clanfield. Because of his poor memory – Allen can usually only remember things for 48 hours – he forgets people's names and faces. Before Endal came into his life, Allen was too embarrassed to go out much or talk to friends who could remember him even though he had no idea who they were. 'Now, they come up to talk about Endal, and even if I don't know who they are, Endal provides a talking point. They stroke and chat, which helps me to socialise again.'

Endal has also helped Allen's marriage and the relationship with his children Liam, now 16, and Zoe, 15. 'They all love him even though Endal very obviously prefers me! He

23

sleeps on my side of the bed, touching my wheelchair with his paw. And when Sandra and I sit on the sofa, watching television, he jumps up between us.'

Sandra, an amazing woman who has put up with more than most wives would cope with, accepts this. 'Life will never be the same again but thanks to Endal, Allen has a second chance – and so do we. Out of eighty seriously injured married men in the Gulf War, only eight marriages survived. Ours is one of them. The children lost their old dad but now Endal has given them a new one.'

Allen and Endal's daily routine illustrates this. Endal wakes Allen every morning, without fail, at 7 am – even when he wants a lie-in. Sometimes Allen tries to keep his eyes closed, pretending he's asleep, but one small gesture to signify otherwise, and Endal is on the bed! He pulls the wheelchair towards Allen's side, using the purple cord that hangs from the back for this purpose. Everything that needs opening in the Parton household has a 'tug' on it like this; purple is Endal's favourite colour. Endal will then put up the loo seat for Allen, using his nose and, like a typical male, fails to put it down again after use! He then helps Allen dress, by opening his underwear drawer and pulling out clean socks and pants. Although there are obvious limits on how far Endal can 'dress' Allen, he can get his clothes and even manages zips on cardigans.

Downstairs, following Allen on his bottom, Allen says 'cereal' and Endal opens a floor-level cupboard and noses out a packet of cereal, which he hands to his master in the chair. All this helps Sandra who is busy getting herself ready for work as Puppy Parent Co-ordinator at the Canine Partners centre. During the morning, Allen will either go with Sandra to the centre to talk to other potential dog recipients or he'll answer Endal's e-mails, which average fifty to a hundred every day, often as a spin-off from Endal's own website. Together, they also manage basic household tasks such as tidying up the sitting room, turning off lights, collecting the post and putting food back in the cupboard.

Towards lunch, the couple often amble down to the local shop where Endal in his red coat and Allen in his chair are a familiar sight. Using his nose, Endal proves to be as good a shopper as any housewife. 'Soup!' commands Allen, and, on cue, Endal will nose out a tin of tomato (one of Allen's favourite) to hand to his master. One day, at a photoshoot, Allen was meant to have asked him for rolls but, being word blind at times, said 'bread' instead. Endal glanced at him and then at the crew and went to the end of the aisle and got the bread like a true professional! Sometimes, as a treat, Allen will ask Endal to 'pick' a Lucky Dip card. So far he's won forty pounds.

When negotiating busy streets, Endal will sit firmly on the pavement if a car is coming, to prevent his master from crossing. Allen's short-term memory means that he can forget to look, and the first time that Endal refused to budge, Allen thought he was being difficult. Then he realised that Endal was trying to warn him that a red car had just come round the roundabout. The car had in fact stopped for the pair but another car might have carried on. At the chemist, Allen will often wait outside in his chair while Endal goes in, wallet in his mouth, to collect Allen's prescription. In fact, Endal is Allen's best medicine as shown when passers-by pause to admire his beautiful golden coat and permanent grin. 'He breaks the ice,' explains Allen. 'Before he came into my life, I wouldn't talk to people. But I'd have to be pretty miserable to ignore someone who likes my dog.'

Back for lunch and Endal hands Allen a plate of sandwiches, which Sandra has made earlier. In the afternoon, it's off to the park to play or perhaps catch up on a bit of television. If one of Allen's legs happens to slip out of his chair, Endal will gently pick up the trousers hem in his mouth and put it back.

At least once a week, if not more, Allen and Endal make guest appearances on television or charity events. During the last one and a half years, Endal – ever the willing performer – has entertained 98 film crews and is possibly Canine

Partners' most famous dog. Endal has also won a string of awards including Dog of the Millennium, Golden Bone Dog of the Year, Assistance Dog of the Year 2001 and Pro-dog Dog of the Year Gold Medal as well as being the first dog to be given a 'Lifetime Achievement Award'. He has been on television from Japan to Australia and has appeared on *Dogs with Jobs*, a television programme shown in the USA and Canada.

But besides relishing the spotlight, Endal has a kind heart and an uncanny knack for spotting people who need special help. He is particularly good at bringing out autistic children, and during a recent trip, made a little boy smile for the very first time. Just as miraculous, he met a five-year-old girl with cerebral palsy. Allen, worried that Endal might knock her over with an over-enthusiastic lick, asked her to sit up straight in her wheelchair instead of leaning to one side. 'She can't do that on her own,' said her mother – and then stopped in amazement. Her daughter, desperate to see this 'miracle dog', had managed to ease herself into an upright position so she could cradle Endal in her arms. There wasn't a dry eye in the room.

Allen, who started public speaking 18 months ago, also visits injured men and women who are still coming to terms with their disabilities. One of his toughest watersheds was to go back to RAF Headley Court, the Epsom-based military rehabilitation centre where Allen had been in dark depths of despair after the accident. 'I couldn't have walked through those doors without Endal but when we did, it was as though I had exorcised all my demons.'

There, Allen and Endal met a young man who was paralysed from his head downwards after jumping into a swimming pool. 'That was me, ten years ago,' said Allen. 'So I told him about Endal and the joy he had brought me. Hopefully, that man will find his own "Endal" in life. I also hope my experience will help people find their own Canine Partners.'

No dog, however, could be exactly like Endal. Not only is

he intelligent and perceptive but he also has character. Take his daily walk to the shops when, after being released from his lead to sniff the local green, he simply had to dash off to sniff a cat. Then there was last Christmas, when he couldn't resist helping himself to a few turkey titbits by opening the fridge door. Weekly weighing sessions on Monday, however, ensure that Endal is not allowed too many illicit snacks. If he's a jot over his average weight of 31 kilograms, it's smaller portions to make sure that he's fit enough to do his job. Thankfully, Endal's arthritis seems to be in remission, and he has regular six-month check-ups at the vet.

Endal himself hates to be parted from Allen. When he and Sandra took a skiing holiday recently, Endal had to go to kennels. As Allen picked him up, he gave him a muted lick but as soon as they got home and closed the front door, he leapt up at him with slobbery kisses. 'Men like us dislike public shows of affection,' jokes Allen.

Endal is also a well-seasoned traveller and a regular on the trains when travelling with Allen to charity events or television studios. The railway service reserves two seats for them. Once, when delayed at Waterloo, Endal put on an impromptu show of fetching and carrying for commuters who were reluctant to leave, even when their train arrived.

But what about the future? 'Most Canine Partners retire after about ten years but I'm going to ask if I can keep him,' says Allen firmly. 'I couldn't imagine another dog. After all, he's my Be All and End All.'

ILYA *and* DIANA

Every year, Barbara Hague and her husband, David, welcome a group of Chernobyl children to their home near Petersfield in Hampshire, to give them a fort-night's holiday. Although the Chernobyl disaster happened in 1986, the effects are ongoing. Some of the children have, or have had, leukaemia while others have different kinds of cancers, although you wouldn't guess it from their smiling faces and their excitement at visiting Britain. But for one recent group of eight- to sixteen-year-olds, the highlight of their visit was sharing a house with Ilya.

Ilya is a Labradoodledolly – a cross between a Labrador, a poodle and a collie – and at the time of these children's visits, he was living with the Hagues who were puppy parenting him for a year. 'Ilya was born during the *I* group of puppies so we called him Ilya after one of the Russian organisers,' explains Barbara. 'The children thought it was wonderful to find a puppy with a Russian name. Even those who weren't used to animals loved cuddling and stroking him; it made them feel less homesick.'

Ilya greatly amused these small visitors with his inquisitive personality, which meant he couldn't resist poking his big black nose into everything. Although his father was a pure white standard poodle, Ilya took after his black Labrador/collie mother with her big body and curly coat. Labradoodles are especially bred to combine the well-known intelligence and sensitivity of a poodle and the retrieving ability and robustness of a Labrador. Ilya's breeder donated him to Canine Partners at seven weeks, but even at that early age, Ilya showed promise. 'He would watch someone and think I can do that too,' recalls Barbara. 'So he'd try to copy all kinds of people – and even other animals. We have a cat, and Ilya used to watch her enviously as she jumped up on garden walls. One day, I caught him climbing up the chicken-wire walls of his toilet area in our garden. He got about six feet up and had to be helped down.'

One of Ilya's brothers, Dooley, was taken on as a pet by Vanessa, another puppy parent who, by coincidence, lived nearby. Barbara and Vanessa frequently got together and the brothers struck up a close bond. One day, when Vanessa and Dooley went home, Ilya ran after their car, trying to get in because he thought he'd been left behind. And on another occasion, when Vanessa came to visit without her dog, Ilya jumped into the back of her car, sniffing under blankets and trying to find his brother.

If Ilya were human, he'd be the kind of person who simply can't sit still or relax on the sofa for more than five minutes. Ilya's inquisitive nature made him the ideal candidate to become a Canine Partner. During puppy class, he was obviously thoughtful and soon learned to respond to commands. One of the things that makes Canine Partners so special is Nina's unique Puppy Education System of component behaviour training and errorless learning, which concentrates on praising a puppy for what it does right and ignoring 'wrong' behaviour. In order to do this, the dog has to be naturally inquisitive and bright as well as ready to take on challenges, which is why Nina's selection procedure is so important. Training starts as soon as the puppy comes to Canine Partners and is taken on by a puppy parent. The latter acts as a sort of foster parent, but besides providing a warm, friendly home, the puppy parent also brings the puppy to weekly Canine Partners classes where it is taught obedient responses, and then practises these commands at home with the puppy.

As the weeks go by, these commands and classes become more complicated. For example, puppies are taught to put their heads through a collar and lead or to come to their owners when called. Similarly, another vital exercise is learning how to turn on large electrical switches; this could be very useful for future partners who might find it difficult to reach light switches. A puppy might start by approaching the switch out of curiosity and then sniff it. This behaviour is immediately 'marked' with a sound from the clicker machine (a small hand-held plastic box that makes a clicking sound when pressed) and the dog is given a small edible treat at the same time. The clicker, along with a treat such as a big cuddle or something nice to eat reinforces positive behaviour. Once the puppy is reliably touching the object with the nose, the trainer stops giving treats and making a clicker noise. The puppy then gets frustrated (where is that clicking noise and that delicious nibble?) and will paw at the switch. Great! Time for the clicker and the treat.

When, after several sessions, the puppy becomes confident at pawing at the switch, the trainer goes back to concentrating on the nose action and giving it a name, 'touch'. With practice, the puppy learns to associate the world 'touch' with turning the switch on with his nose. The puppy is then encouraged to use his paw for the same action, and again, a name is given for that action. The same happens for using the mouth too. That way, puppies are taught to use their mouths, noses or feet to solve different problems. The method also encourages puppies to keep trying in new situations, something that is essential in an assistance dog. It's this kind of dogged determination to get there that makes Canine Partners dogs so special. After all, there aren't many dogs like Ilya who can go into a dark room and turn on a light switch or pass washing out of a laundry basket so his partner can hang it on the line!

After nine to fourteen months with a puppy parent, a puppy comes into the training centre for intensive training for three months or more. By then, a puppy will have graduated to more complex tasks such as opening cupboards or drawers. This could be vital for a future human partner who might need to get a packet of cereal from a bottom cupboard but not be able to reach. A trained assistance dog could tug open the cupboard door, pick up the packet in his mouth and carry it to its owner.

Ilya proved a dab hand (or rather, paw) at most of his exercises. But he was also strong-minded, another characteristic of some Labradoodles. If he wanted to do something, he would. But if he didn't, he'd flash the trainer a charming smile, wag his tail and pretend he hadn't heard her. Nina could tell that he needed someone who appreciated his intelligence but was also determined enough to show Ilya exactly who was boss. Nina's skill in making these matches is legendary; she could be the Cilla Black of a canine *Blind Date* show. Nina, who gives training seminars all over the world, attributes her knack of pairing the right dog with the right person to a combination of factors. As an actress in her early days, she learned to watch people carefully and judge how they interacted. She also has the ability to understand animals as well as humans. From the time she first sees a puppy, she watches it, acutely observing every move. During the weekly training sessions, she will immediately take in whether that puppy has been learning its lessons with its puppy parent or whether it needs a bit of extra help. At the same time, she will work out how that dog's mind ticks. A clever but boisterous dog might not be right for a wheelchair-user who isn't strong enough, either mentally or physically, to take the leading role. But that dog might work for someone who seems physically weak yet has a firm approach that the dog would respect.

Meanwhile, hundreds of miles away in the middle of remote Derbyshire countryside, a small but determined woman was struggling to come to terms with life. Diana Singleton was a 47-year-old seemingly healthy occupational therapist with a husband and two teenage children when she began to feel an odd weakness in her right leg. To begin with, she ignored it, hoping it would go away, and didn't tell anyone, including her husband, Keith. But the sensation got worse, and reluctantly, Diana went to the doctor who referred her to a neurologist. As an occupational therapist, Diana feared the worst. Her condition was similar to multiple sclerosis although it didn't quite fit the pattern. The neurologist, too, was uncertain and sent her to another specialist. No one seemed to know exactly what it was; all they could be certain of was that this mystery disease was attacking her central nervous system. It was also gradually progressive; although she could walk now, Diana would have to use a wheelchair or electric scooter in the future.

The shock hit the Singleton family badly, although ironically, it was Diana who remained calm. She tried to carry on working even though she found it increasingly difficult to visit clients. Keith, who was then working in the engineering industry, took time off to drive her to her office and help her up stairs. But three years ago, Diana decided to take early retirement. Meanwhile, the family had had all kinds of problems including the unexpected death of Keith's father. The shock of Diana's illness and the strain of being a full-time carer took its toll on Keith's emotional health too, and he had to retire on medical grounds.

Then, four years ago, the family visited the Mobility Road Show in Crowthorne, Berkshire. They had taken their

specially adapted caravan, which was one of their few life-
lines, allowing them, like many other disabled couples, to
break out of the restraints that disability had imposed. The
Singletons visited the Canine Partners stand and were deeply
impressed. But at the time, they had a much-loved 15-year-
old Labrador called Dolly. It wouldn't be fair, Diana decided,
to introduce a new animal into the household.

Within a year, however, Dolly had died and Diana kept
thinking about those wonderful Canine Partners dogs who
could do such marvellous things. Rather hesitantly, she
started to fill in the application form, which she had taken
away from the show and had carefully kept. 'I knew there
would be lots of other applicants so I felt I had to "sell
myself" to them. But how?' Diana decided that the best way
was to describe her daily routine and explain how frustrating
it was. She told them how Keith had to help her dress and
that during the morning, she would spend time at her
computer, designing cards or writing letters. If she dropped
her computer pen, which she has to use, as her fingers aren't
strong enough to press the keys, she would have to stop until
someone picked it up. If Keith was out, she might have to
wait an hour or more. In the meantime, Diana would sit and
look at this wretched pen, feeling very frustrated because a
few years earlier, she'd have picked it up without thinking
twice. It was also annoying to go to the front door and find
the post on the floor. 'I'd be able to see a letter I'd been waiting for but be unable to pick it up. It was demeaning and it
made me feel powerless. For someone else, it might be like
losing their voice through laryngitis and not being able to tell
someone what they wanted. Yet most people get their voices
back within days and I knew my disability was permanent
and slowly progressive.'

A few weeks after sending off her application form, Diana
was asked to come down to Petersfield for a day assessment.
This wasn't easy. The Singletons live in a remote village
amidst rolling, rocky Derbyshire moors. The drive down to
Petersfield would take at least five hours; so she and Keith

decided to take the caravan and make a week's holiday out of it. But this was in the winter of 2000 and they didn't know that Britain was about to be hit by torrential floods. It was a hazardous journey through the driving rain, and at times, both wondered if they were doing the right thing.

But when they finally arrived safe and sound, Diana and Keith joined the assessment session, held at the Canine Partners centre, two converted chicken sheds, on an industrial site. Diana was immediately struck by a beautiful chocolate Labrador called Hamish, but was warned by Nina not to take a fancy to any particular dog in case she was disappointed. She also practised basic commands such as 'Sit' with Jinx, a golden retriever. And then she was given Ilya's lead. 'I was told that he had had extra-advanced training because he'd been quite lively. But he didn't seem lively to me. He did everything I asked but it was as though his heart wasn't in it. Something didn't seem right.'

As an occupational therapist, Diana had had extensive experience in understanding how people ticked. Now, she was applying her experience to Ilya and had, quite rightly, worked out that something was amiss. Unknown to Diana, Ilya had refused to work for anyone else that day but, amazingly, he was doing it for her, even if he didn't have a smile on his face. As happens time and time again at Canine Partners, it was the dog who was picking the person he wanted to spend the rest of his life with and not the person picking the dog. But Diana was still troubled; why didn't this dog seem happier?

In the January of the following year, Diana was asked back for a two-day assessment course in the Lake District. Ilya was also there and she could immediately tell that he was working more willingly. No one really seemed to know why, although Nina had her own theory. Could it be that Ilya had finally found someone he could be happy with? Together Diana and Ilya practised off-lead work and walking to heel. But Diana herself was finding the two days very stressful. 'When you have a disability, there's a certain security in knowing the routine and having familiar things around you. But when you're somewhere strange, the bed is the wrong height for getting in and out and you worry about whether you'll need the bathroom in the night.'

Then disaster struck. On the second day, Diana was on her scooter holding on to Ilya's lead when one of the trainers came in. Unexpectedly, Ilya lunged forwards to greet her, pulling Diana out of her chair. 'My leg, my leg!' she cried out. Nina rushed to help. Later she asked, 'Why didn't you tell him to stop, or at least let go of the lead?'

A doctor confirmed that Diana had sprained her ankle and that it had to be strapped up for over three weeks. It would have been enough to have put many people off but not Diana, who blamed herself for not letting go of the lead as she had been taught. So when Canine Partners invited her back for a two-week course to see if there was a good canine match for her, Diana leapt at the chance. She also hoped Ilya would be there. The accident hadn't been his fault, and during those two days, she had become quite fond of this large, friendly, curly-haired dog.

The 12-day course was meant to be held in the Lake District, but due to the foot and mouth outbreak at that time, it was moved to a village near Matlock in Derbyshire. Unfortunately, there wasn't anywhere for Diana and the other people on the course to stay. So instead, Diana and Keith travelled daily from home and Ilya came back every night with Diana as part of the 'getting-to-know-you' exercise. It seemed very strange for the Singletons to have a dog in the house after three years, and Diana allowed Ilya to sniff his way around. 'I had been told to keep him attached to my scooter, like an umbilical cord, so he felt safe. But he didn't eat his dinner that night, presumably because he was nervous.'

During the course, Diana and Ilya practised Canine Partners' extensive range of commands such as 'Get the glove, bring it here' and 'Head through', which tells the dog to put his head through the collar that's held out to him.

Then came the shopping tests in Matlock. Ilya did all the things he was meant to, such as handing over Diana's purse at the counter. But when it came to the lift, he refused to obey Diana's command to press the Call button. 'He just wagged his tail, grinned and ignored me. The trainers weren't allowed to help and I didn't know what to do.' Desperately, Diana tried to divert him with his favourite squeaky toy before repeating the command but still Ilya wasn't playing ball. Diana tried to remember what her training had taught her to do in situations like this – turn away and start the exercise again. That was it! She would take Ilya round the centre again and then back to the lift. Hopefully, he might have a different approach the next time. To her relief it worked, and Diana and Ilya graduated the next day. Finally Diana could take him home. 'But I was still worried. This dog had cost £5000 to train and other people had spent two years to get him to this standard. Would I do him justice?'

Diana soon learned that although Ilya was deeply affectionate and friendly, he also has a stubborn streak with a mind of his own and a lively sense of humour. The trick was to be firm and ensure she was in a position of authority at the start of any working session or else he would do what he wanted. Diana admits that she rather likes that bit of spirit in him. 'It keeps me on my toes so I have to think one jump ahead.'

Ilya certainly caused a stir in Diana's small village; everyone wanted to say hello to the new arrival although Diana had to explain that, as a working dog, he couldn't be touched. The local cub group recently came round for a talk and demonstration; they asked questions like 'What is his favourite command?' The answer is 'Okay', which means Ilya can start eating his meal!

Diana has also learned the joy of looking after Ilya on a one-to-one basis. She is solely responsible for his grooming, feeding, daily exercise and so on. 'As a mum, I've found it very hard not being able to do many of the things that only mums might think of, because of my condition. Caring for Ilya helps to make up for that.'

Although Diana's children, James and Kate, are now 24 and 26, they still frequently come home and they too love having a dog around the house. Ilya's inquisitive personality and sense of fun introduces a note of lightness into a house that has had so much to cope with. Recently, Diana came downstairs in the morning to find that Ilya had opened a cupboard and tucked into a packet of porridge. He also loves fetching the post and recently went a bite too far and chewed two of Kate's letters. Ilya is also very quick on the uptake; when Diana took him to a christening, he stood up with the rest of the congregation during the hymns and then sat when everyone else did. He's also learned to bring Diana's walking frame to her by tugging at the cord, which Keith has tied on the bottom. And he's learned to open the garden gate by tugging on the tennis ball attached to the gate spring, specifically for this purpose. Small achievements like this have made the world of difference to Diana's life. When her mystery illness first struck, she felt deeply frustrated at not being able to continue her active life. But Ilya's amazing ability to open gates, pick up those unreachable keys and pull off her socks when Diana doesn't have the strength to do it herself, has restored some of her dignity. She's no longer totally reliant on her husband or some other kind person to help her. She and Ilya can do it themselves.

During the day, Diana loves the special one-to-one time that she and Ilya enjoy during their walks around the village and along a local river, where the council has recently made a path that's accessible to wheelchairs and pushchairs. But she is careful not to let Ilya get too boisterous in case he tips her out again. Last summer, in the garden when friends were visiting with dogs, Ilya knocked over Diana's scooter when trying to get a treat that the other dogs had. 'I wasn't hurt but I was a bit shaken. Still, dogs are only human.'

Alison Keeling, a Canine Partners trainer, has made several follow-up visits and helped Diana solve minor problems. 'I couldn't stop Ilya from chewing on sticks in the garden and I was worried they might be bad for him. Alison threw some training discs on the ground next to him, which startled him. It's a way of saying that this is not acceptable behaviour and that the dog has to stop. It must have worked because he hasn't done it since.'

Diana has also kept in touch with Barbara, Ilya's puppy parent. The following extracts from Diana's letters to Barbara show just how much Ilya means to her. 'Thank you so much for my superb companion, staunch friend, confidante, helpmate, counsellor, enabler, sounding board, comfort cushion, voice trainer and general all-round good egg and right-hand man! Ilya is a gem. I have fallen for him hook, line and sinker. He's settled in so happily, seems to relish living in a house, is such a delightful character and also a great comedian. There's never a dull moment in the house now and everyone who comes, can't believe what he can do. No one has heard of Canine Partners in this area so there's a lot of interest developing.'

Barbara, too, will never forget the little puppy she fostered for a year. Recently she rang Diana for a chat and 'spoke' to Ilya on the phone when Diana asked him to bark down the phone. 'It was the first telephone conversation I have ever had with a dog!' she said.

Diana and Ilya have also taken up agility classes where Ilya scales six-foot frames with ease, walks the plank and weaves in and out of poles. 'It's lovely for me because I was a very active and athletic person until my disability started. Now I almost feel as though I am flying along with him. I shall have to invest in a turbo-powered scooter!'

During their quiet times at home, Diana talks to Ilya and will confide her feelings of frustration about her illness. She'll tell him if it's a bad day or if she's fed up because she can no longer jog down to the postbox. Maybe she'll tell him if Kate has written that morning and share her excitement about James coming home next weekend. As Ilya looks up at her, taking in every word, it's almost like talking to a best friend or even a counsellor; Ilya's sympathetic face indicates that he understands perfectly. 'I am never alone when Ilya is here,' says Diana firmly. 'It's a wonderful warm feeling.'

But perhaps the final word should come from one of her most recent letters to Barbara and the Canine Partners trainers. 'Ilya is wonderful. He has given me a new lease of life; boredom and a feeling of worthlessness are now a thing of the past. What an exciting adventure we have in front of us. Ilya and I thank you all from the bottom of our hearts.'

INCA *and* DAVID

Beanbag, the little eight-week-old puppy, had an un-happy start in life. Only two days earlier, he had been bought as a surprise present by a young man for his girlfriend. But, like many working couples, they couldn't cope with a lively dog so they had brought him to the local RSPCA to be re-homed. Poor Beanbag looked forlorn and confused as the pair handed him over. Having just got used to one home with its comfy sitting room, he was now being sent to another, which was very different with its rows of dogs, barking in cages. It was a dreadful disruption for such a small puppy who simply wanted a home of his own.

As it was just before Christmas, 49-year-old Helen Freeson, who worked at the RSPCA refuse centre in Gosport, knew she'd have no problem in finding a home for such a handsome puppy, whose honey and platinum blond coat glistened like pure silk. But the problem was that anyone who did take him would probably return him soon afterwards, just as the young couple had done, because of his excitable nature. Beanbag (a cross between a golden retriever and a German shepherd) was like a hyperactive child, always rushing around and demanding one-to-one attention. Not everyone can give this to a dog, especially if there are small children in the family. Helen's instinct told her that this was a highly intelligent dog. 'He would look up at me as he walked beside me, asking for directions. He loved retrieving games and would always hand toys over instead of hanging on to them. Although he was good with other dogs, he was a "people-dog" first and foremost. You don't always get dogs of this calibre.'

Because of these inherent skills, Helen contacted Canine Partners – which she knew about through her work – to see if Nina Bondarenko would like to test Beanbag for work as an assistance dog. Nina asked if she could bring a representative from Meridian TV, which was filming a new series of *Pet Rescue*, the Channel 4 programme about the RSPCA's work. Meridian then wished to film Beanbag being tested for the Canine Partners programme. If he failed, it would be a story, and if he passed, it would be an even better one.

Nina's first impressions of this pretty but enormous dog (he weighed 7 kilos at only four months) were positive. 'He came skipping along the path to greet me and seemed very pleased to see people. He was all smiles with lots of eye contact and was a real charmer. We did all the usual tests such as bombarding him with noises ranging from traffic to clapping but these didn't unnerve him. He also brought over toys and didn't mind if he was left on his own for a while.'

But something wasn't right. 'He reacted beautifully but he was a bit too excitable,' recalled Nina. 'This can be too much for some people, especially if they're disabled. I really wasn't sure, yet at the same time, I didn't want to pass on a dog that had so much potential. So we agreed to take him on trial and find a puppy parent who would look after him while we trained him.'

The puppy parent had an old mixed-breed dog of her own. Although this doesn't normally present problems with

Canine Partners dogs, Beanbag – who was now renamed Inca after his beautiful golden coat – would stand and bark at it. This might have been acceptable for a couple of minutes but Inca wouldn't stop! Even in class, Inca was difficult to train, mainly because he couldn't concentrate. As Nina explains, 'He would start a task, like fetching keys, and then stop, drop them and run after something else. He also pulled impulsively on the lead so the poor puppy parent really struggled with him sometimes.'

Puppies start classes at Canine Partners from the age of seven weeks and they come into the centre, bright-eyed and bouncy, ready to learn. 'Puppies are like blotting paper; they absorb every new experience in class,' says Nina, who has developed the unique Puppy Education System, teaching them how to use their noses, mouths and feet to solve problems such as how to pull on a cord in order to open a drawer. Rewards such as play, food and toys are used to encourage puppies to experiment with different objects. It's called 'errorless learning' because everything useful is reinforced with reward, and any behaviour that isn't useful is usually ignored. But even so, Nina was worried because Inca seemed like a hyperactive child. Something wasn't adding up and she didn't know what.

Meanwhile, Meridian wanted to film Inca in the shops. 'He was nearly ten months old now and still not ready even though he should have been doing jobs like this at six months,' said Nina. 'We gave it a go but he'd pick up a tin and drop it before handing it over. At the till, he'd start to hand over the wallet to the cashier and then drop it, as though he'd suddenly thought about something else. We'd all go, "Oh no, not again Inca!" I call it "spin out" because he was constantly spinning around, starting one thing and then going on to the next before the first was finished. It was also very depressing because we wanted him to succeed.'

Then Nina happened to attend an American conference that highlighted a new test for thyroid deficiencies. Strangely enough, golden retrievers and German shepherds are particularly vulnerable. Nina promptly despatched a blood sample from Inca to the USA and the results showed that he had a significant thyroid deficiency. 'We put him on the appropriate medication and the change was miraculous. Overnight, he was a different dog,' said Nina. 'He did all the tasks perfectly, which showed that he had taken it all in but been unable to finish them physically because of his condition. He also stopped barking so hysterically at other dogs.'

But Inca's problems weren't over yet. The vital medication was expensive – about £30 a week. He would also need a partner who was able, despite his or her own disabilities, to give him the tablets daily. Technically, his condition could have disqualified him from Canine Partners, but on the other hand, he was doing such a good job now he was on his tablets. So they decided to wait to see if the right person came along. If not, he would have to be dropped from the programme and re-housed either through the RSPCA or through one of Canine Partners' contacts.

But all was not lost. After Inca began to improve on his new tablets and was progressing well in advanced training, a new group of men and women – all with varying degrees of disability – arrived at the Canine Partners headquarters in Petersfield in Hampshire. As was usual, they were there for a day as part of their assessment and to see how they interacted with each other and the dogs. Canine Partners prefers to try them out with a variety of dogs to see who gels and who doesn't. One of the group was an amputee called David Beard who had badly damaged his legs after a diving accident in the Indian Ocean during the 1970s. Although he had been born in England, David had worked all over the world and, at the time of his injury, was an assistant harbour master in Australia. He desperately wanted to continue his job but was in agonising pain with the leg ulcers that had developed from the accident, so in 1999, he returned to England for what he thought would be 'proper' medical help. But by a cruel twist of fate, while in hospital he developed MRSA (methicillin resistant staphylococcus aureus, the so-called flesh-eating bug) and had to have both legs amputated above the knee.

'I told myself that I would cope but inside I must have been very angry,' admits David, a well-built man in his early sixties. 'I had been divorced for years and my children are grown up and living in New Zealand. All I wanted was to work abroad again in the sun but now was unable to. Social services asked me where I wanted to live so I said "Anywhere, providing it's not in a town."'

By some stroke of luck, David was relocated to an adapted bungalow in Blakesdown, Worcestershire, which happened to be excellent dog-walking country even though this was the last thought on David's mind. 'I shut myself away in the bungalow and went out as little as possible. The television was one of the few things that kept me going. To be honest, I was a grumpy recluse.' Amazingly, television turned out to be David's saving grace. Two months after moving in, David watched a programme in which Esther Rantzen interviewed Allen Parton and Endal. 'Suddenly, for the first time in years, I felt a buzz. I picked up the phone, tracked down Canine Partners and asked how I could apply for a dog too.'

However, it was a lengthy process and it was another four months before a representative from Canine Partners visited David to interview him and find out if he – and his home – were suitable for a dog. For example, a Canine Partner can only go to a recipient who owns a garden, and, luckily, David's bungalow has one, although it's not large.

David was then invited to attend the first of a series of assessment days at the training centre in Petersfield, Hampshire. During one of the exercises, the participants were asked to call their assigned dog back from playing with the other dogs in the paddock. It's hard work because there hasn't been much time to forge a bond, and not many succeed. Certainly, David, with his scowl and sarcastic manner, didn't seem the kind of man to attract friends, either the two- or four-legged variety. But Inca could see something that no one else could. Although he usually loved racing round the paddock, he sat down and stared long and hard at David with searching eyes. 'I know you, I want to be your friend,' he seemed to say. Nina had never seen him like that with anyone before. Something was definitely beginning to happen.

Back at the centre, David and the others worked with the different dogs, tackling exercises such as getting safely into a car, crossing the road and retrieving dropped items. When David came back to his original spot in the waiting area, Inca was taking a short nap behind a sofa. But he woke up as soon as he heard David speak. Putting both front paws on top of the sofa, Inca craned his neck towards his new friend and, wagging his tail frantically, barked and whined as though to say, 'I'm here, don't go past me!' David wheeled himself up and said 'Oh there you are, my little cloth-eared puppy.' It was a sign that the two might be a perfect match.

However, there were several hurdles to be crossed. David, along with the other applicants, was called back for two more days on successive months. Again, he was 'tried out' with other dogs. As Nina explained, if you set someone up with one dog from the beginning and it doesn't work out, it's very hard for that person to transfer his or her affections to another dog. It's like looking for a comfortable pair of shoes. If you keep trying, you'll find one that's a perfect fit.

After what was to have been a day visit, David was asked if he would stay overnight and have another session at the training centre the following day. That agreed, CPI booked David and Inca into the nearby Travelodge. David admits to being a little concerned that, after a day when working with Inca had not been brilliant, he might prove a real handful. Wrong, David! Inca behaved as though he were completely used to such living conditions. When they went down to dinner at the restaurant, Inca put on a star performance, settling down under the table while David ate. He did everything that was asked of him and attracted a great deal of attention from the other diners, who remarked on this wonderful behaviour. That night Inca went to sleep, on his bed at the foot of David's.

But in the night, David woke with phantom pains in his non-existent legs. Such pains had occurred frequently since the operation, as is the case with many amputees. Somehow Inca sensed his new friend was in trouble. 'I felt a bump and then a wriggle, and then suddenly, there was this dog, nestling up to my stumps, licking them,' recalls David. 'Something went click in my head and from that minute on, I haven't had any pain. Instead I joke that, thanks to Inca, I have four perfectly good legs of my own.'

It was nothing short of a miracle. To his joy, David was partnered with Inca. But then the hard work really began. Together, the two began their 12-day residential course during which David had to learn to give commands, and Inca to obey them. They had to learn to work together as a team, and David had to learn how to motivate Inca to respond. One of the biggest challenges for Inca was to walk sedately on the lead beside David's scooter, without chasing rabbits or being distracted.

Nor did David make it easy for himself. Used to being independent all his life, David now found it difficult to be part of a group. He would make excuses to avoid being with the others, he would arrive late and he tended to go off by himself. After several days of this, Nina had to get tough. Taking him to one side, she told him in no uncertain terms that if he wanted this dog, he had to work at it. Otherwise, he wouldn't be allowed to stay.

It was the catalyst that David needed. He wanted Inca and Inca seemed to want him, although why, David couldn't quite understand. But whatever the reason, David had to pull himself together and follow the rules. From that moment on, he made a heroic effort to do what he was told, keeping his fingers crossed that Canine Partners would finally team him up with this amazing dog who had chosen him above all the odds. Inca, too had his paws crossed. By the end of those 12 days, Inca knew nearly a hundred commands, ranging from 'Sit' and 'Stay' to 'Find my door keys'.

Inca, like all the other dogs, had to complete a final test in the 'real world'. This involves a series of tasks that must be fulfilled by dog and person together in a shopping centre. David and Inca went to Horsham. 'It was quite scary because we had to cross the road, use the lift in a department store and go shopping, knowing that all over town there were hidden Canine Partners observers who were checking that we were doing it right,' says David. 'I was sweating with apprehension in case anything went wrong but Inca was incredible. He didn't put a paw wrong.' That August, David and Inca were part of the Canine Partners graduation ceremony. It hadn't been an easy feat. 'Not everyone who applies for a dog ends up with one,' explains Heather Caird, training centre manager. 'We don't want to give a percentage for the success rate in case it puts anyone off. But we go to a great deal of trouble to make sure that both the dogs and the owners are compatible.'

Last July was David and Inca's first anniversary, and to celebrate, Inca did all his favourite things: a two-mile walk in the morning followed by a picnic by a local lake and a boisterous games session in the park where David throws the ball on a rope. Anyone watching Inca leaping four to five feet in the air after his ball can tell that this is an Olympic athlete in action. 'We walk anything between four and fourteen miles a day, often starting at 7 am and sometimes not coming back until dinner,' says David as he pours out a drink for Inca from the water container he carries on his scooter. 'I might not be able to take him sailing but we explore on wheels, instead. The other day, we walked nine miles to Chaddesley Corbett, a village I hadn't been to before. It's not the same as exploring by boat but with Inca, it's almost as good. Before he arrived, strangers used to look first at my stumps and then my eyes. Now they look first at Inca, then my eyes and, sometimes, at my stumps. When Inca is with me, strangers open conversations with me, which was not the case previously.

Inca is definitely an adventurer like David. Recently, they went to London to collect the Animal Planet Award for Best Friend. Nominations are made through videos of dogs and their owners. Canine Partners had nominated David and Inca who were then visited by the organisers and put on the shortlist. Inca had never been on a train before but he took it all in his bound. On arriving at Waterloo, they were met with a sea of legs – a far cry from Blakedown, a small sleepy village. 'He looked at me, shrugged and his eyes seemed to say "Well, I wasn't expecting this but we'll cope" and we did!'

Inca had never been across a stage before in front of hundreds of people but he did it as though he'd been treading the boards all his life. He also displayed the initiative that marks out a good Canine Partner. 'There was nowhere for the dogs to relieve themselves apart from a few stones on top of a concrete block,' recalls Nina, who was also at the ceremony. 'Inca leapt up and with amazing dexterity, did this enormous wee on this tiny patch of stones and then leapt down again.'

Inca's arrival has made a huge difference to David's life, both emotionally and physically. This summer, the pair are planning a 215-mile walk from Blakedown to Weymouth and then by ferry on to Guernsey where David grew up. It's an adventure that David would never have thought possible in those dark days when he was lying in hospital, facing an uncertain future. 'Inca is already in training with his daily walks,' says David. 'It will be the first time he's been on a ferry and although it's not like the huge ships that I'm used to sailing, it will be wonderful. I'm hoping to raise money for Canine Partners, British Legion and Soldiers', Sailors', and Airmen's Families Association. I'm not sure how long it will take but we plan to cover about 15 miles a day with a camper van for overnight. I know Inca will love meeting different people on the way.'

Inca also helps David feel safe. 'Recently, my chair broke down while we were in a wood and it was a great comfort to know he was by my side. He can also do practical things. I usually use a "jungle bar" to heave myself out of bed. It's difficult to sit up when you don't have legs. But when I found it hard one day, I held out a pull rope and he tugged me out of bed. He almost sent me flying across the room! He also found my keys when I lost them the other day. I simply said, "Keys, Inca, find," and he nosed around until he discovered them, hidden behind a table leg. I don't want to sound mushy, but he has given me my life back. He looks after me and I look after him.' Nina agrees. 'Since Inca, David has become a much softer man. He's less critical, generally, and more open.'

This is all down to Inca who has insisted on introducing David to people whom he wouldn't otherwise have met. One of them is Karen, the barmaid at the local 'Old House and Home' where David and Inca often have lunch. Inca's all-time favourite is a bowl of sausages but he waits patiently by the table until David has finished eating. Only then, does he eat the pieces, which David feeds by hand. For pudding, Karen will place a packet of Quavers on the bar counter and, on command, Inca runs up, picks it up and hands it to his master for opening. 'He won't eat any other kind of crisp,' says David. 'And he won't bother running up for an empty packet either!' Like all red-blooded males, Inca also enjoys his food. The secret to his beautifully silky coat and brilliant white teeth is, David firmly believes, his diet of raw meat, pasta and a vegetable sauce that David makes himself. He eats a staggering 800 grams of raw meat a day – one-thirtieth of his body weight. But because of his energetic lifestyle, he remains a slim 30 kilos. Exercise, for Inca, is one of the joys of life – he easily covers 2000 metres a morning just through chasing his ball. If he thinks David has forgotten his walk, he will fetch his jacket and the house keys. He can also recognise the sound of Windows closing down on David's computer and will be jumping around in anticipation of 'Walkies'. When he strained his paw, running after a ball, he still wanted to play. And the most miserable three weeks of his – and David's life – was when the vet insisted that Inca stay in the bungalow for a rest. 'It was like having a child in bed with a broken leg.'

David knows how he feels. Like most land-lugged sailors, he itches to go abroad again. But he couldn't contemplate leaving Inca. 'The government is still trying to sort out passports for dogs; it's not as easy as it looks. And I can't get a passport out myself because I don't actually own Inca. Through the agreement with the charity, I "rent" him for life for a mere one pound. My ambition would be to buy Inca even though he would cost at least £7,000, the cost of his training. And then I'd like to take him back with me to Australia. If that isn't possible, I'd love to go to France. I'm sure Inca would adapt.' As if on cue, Inca grins. 'Sounds great,' he seems to say. 'But if it doesn't work out, we could always do something else. Like order another bowl of those delicious sausages.'

IVORY *and* IAN

'Sit, Ivory, sit!' The beautiful yellow Labrador retriever reluctantly walks back to Ian Free's wheelchair and sits down, his eyes fixed on Ian's face. 'Are you sure?' he seems to be saying. 'Isn't it time for a walk?' Ian shakes his head but can't help smiling. There's no need for him to say anything; the bond between the pair is stronger than words. And it's not surprising; for Ivory is the dog that Ian thought he would never have.

To understand why, we need to go back to 4 July 1986 when Ian, then a 19-year-old strapping six-foot-six lorry driver, had gone down to the local swimming pool in Portishead, near Bristol, with a group of friends. He dived into the deep end as he had done on countless occasions before. But as he did so, he cricked his neck awkwardly without even hitting the bottom. Three weeks later, he woke up in hospital.

Ian realised something was seriously wrong when he saw five doctors surrounding his hospital bed. They told him that his friends had pulled him out of the water and resuscitated him. He'd been rushed to hospital but it was too late. Ian was paralysed from his chest down and had no feeling in his fingers. It was, said the doctors, one of those inexplicable freak accidents. In a split second, Ian had gone from being a sports-mad athletic youth with his whole future in front of him, to a boy who now faced the rest of his life in a wheelchair.

It was more than enough to make many 19-year-olds give up. But Ian's parents, Janet and Robert, adopted a very positive outlook on life and this had rubbed off on their only son. During the following year, which he spent having physiotherapy and rehabilitation at Rookwood Hospital in Cardiff, Ian decided he would live on his own when discharged. 'I'd heard too many horror stories about people being smothered by their family and friends. I didn't want everyone pointing and saying "There's the Frees' son in a wheelchair."'

Within six months of leaving hospital, Ian moved into an adapted bungalow in Portishead, just two miles from his parents and a stone's throw from the swimming pool that had changed his world. But life on his own wasn't easy. This big, broad-shouldered man was itching to get out and about, just as he used to. He even refused to buy an electric wheel-chair because he was determined to use every ounce of strength that he had left to get himself about, rather than relying on a machine. Instead of live-in help, he chose to have two careworkers, provided by the local council, to come in and help twice a day. His parents also visited, but apart from that, he was on his own.

As the months went by, Ian's frustration grew. He was used to going out to the pub or seeing friends whenever he wanted. Before his accident, he had enjoyed a lively social life and had played football, rugby and cricket. Now he was limited to playing specially adapted table tennis. It was a bitter pill for anyone to swallow, especially a man as independent as Ian. Determined not to give up, however, Ian learned to drive a specially adapted vehicle within a year of the accident. It helped, but even so, meeting his friends involved major planning. He could only go out if one of his helpers or parents was around to help him into the car, using the hoist that is stored on the roof, like a roof rack. And, someone then had to hang around while he saw his friends, in order to help him home again. No longer could he make spontaneous decisions to nip down to the pub or go to a party. It was enough to make any man weep, and at times, despite his fiercely positive attitude, Ian did just that.

Then, in 1989, he received an unexpected phone call from Charity Search, a local group that had helped him raise money for a computer. They told him about Canine Partners. Ian, however, knew this wouldn't help him Having grown up with border collies, he was practical enough to know that he couldn't control a dog in a manual wheelchair.

During the next five years, many of Ian's original friends moved away or lost touch. Then in 1994, Ian reluctantly accepted that a manual wheelchair couldn't give him the independence he craved, so he and his parents clubbed together to buy an electric chair for £5500. As soon as he switched it on, Ian tasted the sweet smell of independence for the first time in eight years. All through this time, Ian had never forgotten about the charity that trains dogs. Within a week of getting his chair, he rang Charity Search and they said they would make some phone calls on his behalf. Ten minutes later, the phone rang. It was a woman called Nina Bondarenko. Could she come over for a chat?

'She asked what I liked doing and I told her I enjoyed table tennis and going to the pub and cinema with friends. She also had a look at my garden and asked if I had a dog, would I be able to take him out for a walk, feed and groom him, etc. Because I had grown up with dogs, I knew I could. Nina had also brought a friend who was making a documentary for

Channel 4. She had a course coming up for people who might benefit from assistance dogs and asked if I wanted to come and whether I'd accept being filmed. I replied yes to both questions and then asked when it was happening. Three weeks, she said. I could hardly believe that my world was changing so fast.'

Another date that stands out clearly in Ian's mind is 15 August 1994. Not only was it Ian's twenty-eighth birthday but it was also the day he met Alex. 'There was a film crew, me, two other people in chairs and Nina in a tiny room, not much bigger than my sitting room. We'd just had champagne and cake to celebrate my birthday and then Nina said she'd like to introduce me to the dogs.'

Four golden rockets shot into the room, jumping up with tails wagging and slobbering over everyone in sight. Ian fell immediately for Alex, a beautiful golden retriever who was both super-intelligent and gentle. Almost immediately, this lovely dog seemed to understand that Ian couldn't use his hands. If Ian dropped something during that day of training, Alex would pick it up. Ironically, Alex had one big failing. He loved water. And of course, it was in water where Ian had had his accident. Some people might have seen this as a bad omen but Ian interpreted it as a positive sign. Ian saw other positive signs. The fourth of July, the day Ian became paralysed is Independence Day in the USA. And what is the dog charity called? Canine Partners: Opening Doors to Independence. Just as important, this course was the first that Canine Partners had ever held. Ian and Alex simply had to work out together.

During the training sessions that followed, it certainly looked as though they did. 'You could see that there was a magical bond between them,' said Nina. 'Alex adored Ian; it was almost as though his soft brown eyes were saying "I can see what you've been through and I'm going to make it better for you."'

But there was a huge hurdle to get through before Ian could finally take Alex home. Part of the training sessions involved a big test when the dogs were taken out for on-lead and off-lead training. Fine. Alex was usually spot-on for both. But this time, the dogs were being tested in a car park in East Wittering, right on the coast. Furthermore, the car park was next to the beach. Would Alex be able to resist the temptation of splashing about in the water, which he absolutely adores doing or would he head for the sea and ruin his chances of being paired with Ian?

At the beginning of the session, Alex behaved perfectly. Then came the big test: the 'Down and stay off-lead' exercise, when the dogs had to lie still for five minutes while their owners 'disappeared' before calling them. As Ian headed for a giant bin to hide behind, he knew this was make or break. His heart pounding nineteen to the dozen, he counted the seconds: the five minutes seemed more like a lifetime. Finally, Ian called out 'Come here', and to his huge relief, that golden rocket shot towards him. 'Nina was also standing there, looking down on me with this huge grin on her face. She said, "You know, he ignored the beach and was looking around for you saying 'Where's my Daddy gone?' You two have got something special."'

Alex went home with Ian, and for four years they lived happily together. If this were a fairy story, the tale would end there. But this is real life and as Ian found out on that day he went swimming, life has a way of turning you upside down when you are least expecting it. During those four years, Alex did the usual things that Canine Partners are trained to do. He brought Ian's keys, helped him off with his jacket, unloaded the washing machine, opened cupboards and was a constant faithful companion. Then one day, Ian noticed something that sent a shiver of premonition down his back. 'Alex always slept by my bed, and one morning I saw that when he woke me, he rested his chin on the side of the bed and not his two paws as he usually did. That day, he didn't jump up on the bed, and over the next few days I could tell there was something wrong.'

On Nina's advice, Ian took Alex to the vet who gave the

dog anti-inflammatory treatment, which helped for a few weeks. But Alex still wasn't right, so Ian took him to a specialist for a second opinion. Within five minutes, the specialist announced that Alex was in severe pain. An X-ray then revealed that he had a trapped nerve and a chip on his disc. There was only one solution: a major operation. To Ian, this was almost as devastating as his own accident.

To make it worse, Ian himself wasn't well, having just recovered from a pressure sore. It's easy to forget how physically limiting it is to sit all day, every day, in a chair – especially when you're as big as Ian – which is why pressure sores are common problems for people confined to wheel-chairs. After Alex's operation, the vet recommended minimal exercise, which was just as well, bearing in mind Ian's own state of health. Then Ian had a brilliant idea: acupuncture! He took Alex for treatment and he improved two-fold. Slowly, Ian worked on building up Alex's fitness as well as his own, and for a time it looked as though everything would be all right. Unfortunately, Alex was still unable to work at his previous high level – the stretching up and standing put too much strain on his damaged back. Reluctantly, Ian finally accepted the guidance from Nina and Canine Partners, and retired Alex from full-time work. He began to think about allowing a new dog into his life. Around that time, Charlie, another golden retriever, had come back into training from a previous placement. Ian volunteered to take on Charlie as an assistance dog and to keep Alex, who got on well with the other dogs, just as a pet. This seemed the ideal solution because it meant Ian and Alex didn't have to be parted. Initially, Alex found it difficult to 'abdicate' from his usual role. But slowly, over the next few weeks, he learned to let Charlie fetch keys, open cupboards and bring in the post. Ian identified with Alex; both had ill-health that prevented them from doing what they really wanted. It was tough but they had to get on with it.

For a year, it worked well. Then disaster struck again. As a puppy, Charlie had had a bone chip on a front joint. Although this hadn't caused any problems, it did make him more prone to arthritis. One morning, as Charlie was reaching up to open a cupboard, he suddenly pulled up short. 'Surely it can't be happening again?' thought Ian. But it was. Although arthritis might not be serious in a dog that's a pet, it can be disastrous for a working dog who has to be in peak condition to fulfil his duties for a disabled partner. Tests showed that Charlie was developing arthritis, which meant Ian had two disabled dogs on his hands. He knew there was only one course of action. Both dogs had to be re-homed.

All was not totally lost, however. Canine Partners allowed Alex to go to Ian's parents as a pet, which meant that Ian could still see him regularly, while Charlie went to work as a demo dog for a local couple who were fundraisers for Canine Partners. But Ian had gone from a two-dog-owner to a no-dog man. Would he ever find another Alex? To make it worse, the charity didn't even have a dog available at that time who would suit his needs.

Although Ian now had a full-time live-in carer, the house was empty without a dog to talk to or take for walks. When he went to the supermarket without the customary lead attached to the hook on his chair, people would stop him, asking if his dog had died. For two months, Ian struggled on. And then along came Finian. Finian was a chocolate Labrador with personality! Nina had already warned Ian that Finian was impulsive. He was not generally difficult, but whenever he saw another dog, his hackles would go up and he would expand as though he was ready to blow up. 'He might look aggressive but he wasn't,' explained Ian. 'It was just his way of greeting other animals.'

Finian could not have been more different from Alex who had behaved perfectly with other dogs. Even so, Ian agreed to have Finian for six months and see what happened. 'Normally we would introduce dogs to owners through training sessions, but Ian had had more experience than most so it was better doing it this way,' explains Nina. 'Instead, Ian and Finian were going to join us for the last part of the training course.'

The night before, however, something happened that made Ian change his mind. As he took Finian out for his evening walk, he rushed up to another dog, hackles raised to say 'Hello' in his usual wild manner. 'Something inside me said "This isn't good,"' admits Ian. 'I had started to give a lot of talks to the public about Canine Partners and wanted to use Finian as a demo dog. If he saw another dog in the crowd, it would be easy for someone to assume he was aggressive and this would give the charity a bad name.'

Reluctantly, but convinced it was the right action, Ian told Nina his decision, so Nina took him out of the training course. Finian went on to train as a prison sniffer dog but, after failing to make the very tough grades, eventually ended up as a pet to an army sergeant. Meanwhile, Ian was still without a dog, and Nina was acutely aware that he needed a canine friend. 'No one could replace Alex; and after all those other disappointments, it was better to give him a bit of a breather. We had some dogs close to graduation so I asked Ian if he could do us a favour and provide these dogs a taste of what their lives would be like when they were finally placed.'

So for the next six weeks, Ian had a series of canine house guests. First he had Harley, a chocolate Labrador, for two weeks: then Hazel, a golden retriever, for a few days; followed by Hamish, another chocolate Lab, for a fortnight. Then came Hector. Could Hector finally be the dog for Ian and could he ever match up to Alex?

At first, it seemed possible. A flat-coated black retriever, Hector was a very tall, beautiful dog, but there was one big problem. His mind kept wandering, which in human terms, meant he had attention deficiency syndrome. He started doing a job but as he did it, he would think about something else and run off to do it. Alternatively, he might take a tin out of a cupboard to give to Ian and then decided to crush it himself with his teeth and discover what was inside. He would remember commands on some days and forget them on others. For a couple of months Ian persevered, taking

Hector through advanced training with Canine Partners until Nina and he decided they weren't meant to be.

Ian couldn't believe his bad luck. He had gone through almost every case history scenario, and apart from Alex, not one dog had really worked out. For the next eight months, Ian was dog-less and began to wonder, understandably, if it was his fault, even though he had been reassured that it wasn't. Ian desperately missed having a dog as a shadow and a pair of brown eyes following him wherever he went. Understandably, he lost weight and began to feel sorry for himself. Canine Partners were very supportive and suggested he participate in demos with a woman called Jenny whose dog Free had been named after Ian. That helped but it wasn't the same. Then, finally, Nina rang to ask if he wanted to go on the next training course as there might be a dog that was suitable. Ian didn't need to be asked twice!

And that's where Ian finally met his match. As he wheeled himself into the training room, he was immediately struck by two yellow Labrador retriever brothers, Ivory and Icon. 'They were both beautiful dogs; too intelligent for their own good! They obviously thought they were the bees' knees and I couldn't help thinking that if I could get them to do what I wanted, they would be brilliant. It was a bit like taming a beautiful wild horse. If I could do it, great. If not, I'd be back to square one.'

Ian was put to work with Ivory and within minutes they had fallen for each other. As they worked together, Ivory's eyes clicked with Ian's. It was almost as if he knew what Ian was going to ask him before Ian gave the command. Psychologically, Ivory was clearly the equivalent of Ian in human terms – strong-willed, determined and athletic. Both man and dog knew where they were going, and they weren't afraid of saying so. Could this be the match that finally worked?

Nina had a hunch that it might. During the past two years, she had been keeping a close eye on Ivory who, like all Canine Partners' puppies, had been living with a puppy parent. Ivory's foster family, from Emsworth in Hampshire, had been June and Martin Davy and their children – Philip, then 15, Laura, 13, and Sean, 9. All through those two years, Nina had wondered whether Ivory could be Alex's successor. Certainly he had the intelligence to do what Ian asked but he also had the independence that meant he might prefer to do what he wanted to do, rather than what someone else wanted.

Because of this independent streak, Ivory had been quite a challenge for the Davy family. He was their second Canine Partners puppy, and June recalls that he was so independent that for the first nine months he didn't like to be held or even cuddled. 'Instead, he would wriggle and bite until he won, like a hyperactive child. He was a cute-looking puppy with a pink nose and pink pads and a white velvet-like coat and a tail that always stood straight up in the air. We nick-named him Piglet. We concentrated most of his training on basic good manners such as coming to heel, since he found things like opening doors and turning on light switches very easy. Walking him was a real challenge; he would behave beautifully for a time and then suddenly dash into an interesting ditch, pulling us after him. It wasn't until he was about nine months old that he learned real respect for Martin, and then for the rest of us. From then on, providing we were firm, he repaid us with excellent behaviour.'

Ivory also showed his sense of humour from an early age. To celebrate the millennium, the Davys had a small party to which Endal and his owners came. Endal and another dog were kept on leads so people wouldn't fall over them, but Ivory was loose since it was his home. He thought it great fun to put a toy or bone down in front of the other dogs and wait for them to go for it. Because he was off-lead, he was always quicker than they were.

He also continued to do everything at 90 mph. This included opening the children's bedrooms and going in and helping himself to whatever interesting toys he wanted. At puppy classes, he found it hard to sit still and wriggled and barked when bored. Luckily, his behaviour at home was much better. However, Ivory has one Achilles' heel: he hates anyone touching his feet. 'He really dislikes having his nails cut,' says June. 'When he stood on a bee in the garden, he had to go to the vet to have the sting removed. It took three of us to hold him so the vet could look at his paw.'

'He would be too much for many people to handle,' admits Nina. 'But Ian is strong. He's not afraid to say no but he can be gentle with it, just like Ivory. When I first saw Ivory and his brother, I could see that they were very tough and cool. They were like a pair of guys swaggering around town, marching about with oodles of confidence. I admit that I hesitated because they were too confident and pushy and I knew they'd be too much of a handful for many people. But something inside me said they'd be perfect for someone with the right kind of experience.' Ian was that man. 'He has a high level of disability so needs a dog who can think,' says Nina. 'Ivory needs a challenge; he's not a dog to sit around.'

Both Ian and Ivory seem to sense this, which may explain why they bonded immediately during that first training session. 'The pain of the past few years melted away because I finally had a dog with me. I could see that Ivory was too intelligent for his own good but I was also convinced that I could calm him down. Something told me that he and I were made for each other.' To prove the point, Ian dyed his normally brown hair blond to show that he and Ivory were mates. It certainly raised a few laughs during the training session and Ivory's enthusiastic licks suggested that he approved. Because he'd been through this course before, Ian was the more experienced member of the group, often giving advice to the others about their dogs. But Ivory, too, seemed to know what he was doing, despite being a novice. At the end of each day, the group returned to the classroom to go over what they had learned. Ian was told that he and Ivory worked so well together that he could probably teach his dog to do the ironing, organise the washing up and make the coffee. What made this special bond? Ian wasn't sure but he had noticed that Ivory responded faster to his deep, measured and reasonably slow voice than to anyone else's.

So far, so good. But would Ivory and Ian pass the final test at the end of the training course? This time the test was carried out in Horsham shopping centre. Ian took his time, determined not to rush. The exam route involve crossing roads, going into shops, buying things and going into a lift. Although Ian had practised in the classroom, he and Ivory had never been in a real lift, and to his horror, he realised that the shopping centre lift was made of glass. How would Ivory cope when the lift went up and he could look down on the shoppers below? Some people don't like this sensation of height and perhaps Ivory wouldn't either. Ian needn't have worried. Ivory just sat down and seemed to say 'Hmm. This is a nice view.'

The next test was to buy a plastic jug from a shop. Ian didn't envisage any problems because a jug was easy for Ivory to get down from the shelf and easy for him to carry along to the counter. What Ian hadn't banked on was the slippery supermarket floor, which caused Ivory to drop the jug; he then decided it would be a good game to play with it. But Ian was ready. 'Easy,' he said firmly; 'easy' is the command that means 'Get back to work and stop being such a dizzy dog.' He only had to say it once. 'Sorry,' said Ivory. 'Thought it was time to play. All right then, we'll get on with business.' He then carried the jug up to the till, took the wallet from Ian's pocket and handed it over to the till assistant.

Even so, Ian was worried. He'd been through this course before with Alex; everyone expected him to know it all. Supposing he didn't do as well as they expected? It would be terrible to fail at this stage when he had finally found the right dog. In fact, Ian and Ivory passed with flying colours, but experience had taught Ian not to celebrate too soon. They were about to face the next hurdle; going home together. If Ivory behaved as well as he had done on the course, it would be wonderful. But if he didn't, it would be back to square one and Ian wasn't sure he could handle that.

As soon as Ivory got out of the car, he sniffed around and followed Ian through the bungalow to the back door. 'He checked for smells and ran round the garden like a crazy puppy,' says Ian fondly. 'Then he marched back with me to the living room, took a look at his bed and said "So that's where I sleep is it? Good. I'm exhausted!" And he lay down and had a little nap. He wasn't at all nervous. It was as though he knew the house already.'

Ivory has now been with Ian for just over a year and so far their partnership has been a great success. Ian spends most of his time giving demos in support of CPI. According to Ian, Ivory is a total show-off who loves fetching and carrying in front of the crowds. Recently, Ian lost his keys during a demonstration in a park crammed with nearly three thousand people. 'I just said "Find Keys" and we backtracked our steps through the crowds. Amazingly, Ivory picked them up; it was like finding a needle in a haystack. I'm sure that no other dog could have done it.'

Ian says Ivory has given him back his life after so many setbacks. On Ian's command, Ivory 'talks' in dog language, making a variety of noises. He accompanies Ian in his huge Discovery, travelling alongside Ian's carer, a young woman called Mandy, who helps Ian out of the car so he can go to the pub, cinema or a demonstration. Ivory responds instantly to Ian's voice or even a raised eyebrow. A simple 'Down' will have Ivory down on the ground. He might sometimes exhibit the traits of a temperamental film star but when the cameras roll and there's an audience, Ivory always behaves himself. At the pub, he's well known for 'paying' for a meal or drink by handing over Ian's wallet. Sometimes, he'll raise his head as though to say 'I'm here. Please don't forget me.'

Both Ian and Ivory's social life revolves around Canine Partners, where both have made friends. Ivory has a girlfriend called Sable, a Rottweiler who belongs to local neighbours; every time Sable sees a wheelchair, she barks, presuming that Ivory is not far behind. Meanwhile, Ian will never forget Alex, and when his parents visit, they often bring Alex along. At the grand old age of nine, however, he prefers to watch while the younger puppy plays at his feet. 'I never thought I'd say this after Alex, but Ivory is a perfect match. He's so intelligent that he knows what I want to do almost before I give him the command. As a result, he gives me as much independence as I can possibly get in my position. But Alex will always be regarded as my number-one dog. He was the first dog trained by Canine Partners and my first assistance dog.'

For Ian, Ivory arrived just in time. 'I'm not sure if I would have managed without him. I knew it wasn't my fault that the others didn't work out, but it happened once too often. Now, thanks to Ivory, I can go forward instead of back. I owe him a huge debt of gratitude for all he has done for me. He will always be a part of my life.'

FRODO *and* STEPHANIE

When Stephanie Pengelly went on her first blind date, she took someone with her – Frodo, her large chocolate-brown Labrador. Frodo might not seem an average bodyguard but Stephanie trusted his judgement. If her dog liked her date, he would let her know. And if he didn't, she wouldn't bother meeting up with that date again. After all, she couldn't be too careful. Frodo had not been impressed with Stephanie's first five dates. Instead of sitting quietly under the pub table, as he had been taught to do during Canine Partners training, he wriggled about and refused to stay still.

Stephanie was about to give up, but then came her sixth date, whom she had met through an internet dating service.

John, a quietly spoken, kind man, was an instant hit with Frodo. Finally, he was able to relax under that table, knowing that Stephanie was in safe hands; and within six months, he was bringing John his slippers along with Stephanie's, something he always did when his owner walked in through the front door on her crutches.

However, it wasn't always like this. In fact, Stephanie and Frodo themselves were almost one of those blind dates that didn't work out. The story goes back to the summer of 1987 when Stephanie, an attractive vivacious woman, was expecting her third child at the age of 33. Her other two children, Mark, age 9, and Emma, age 11, had been born with what she'd been told was mild cerebral palsy, which was why they both walked with an uneven gait. Just before James was born, Emma felt her legs were getting worse, so Stephanie asked for another consultation at the hospital. To her horror, she was told that Emma and Mark didn't have cerebral palsy at all. Instead, they were suffering from a rare medical condition called hereditary spastic paraparisis. Even worse, they had inherited it from her!

Stephanie had been adopted and had no idea she was carrying this hereditary disease, and she was terrified that her unborn baby would also have it. Stephanie's and her husband's fears were confirmed when tests showed that baby James also carried the disease, although not as strongly as his brother or sister. Meanwhile, Stephanie herself was told that her own health could deteriorate at any time. 'I had always been slightly clumsy, often dropping things, but I had no idea there was something wrong with me. Overnight, all our lives had changed. How would we manage?'

Over the next few years, Stephanie's marriage began to disintegrate, and by the time James was eight, his father had left home. Stephanie found it increasingly hard to walk and had to give up her job as a social worker. Partly for companionship and partly because her children were desperate for a dog, she bought a collie called Lady. The whole family adored her. Stephanie hadn't realised how exuberant collies could be, nevertheless, she carried on trying to take Lady for walks, despite her increasingly infirm legs. Stephanie has always had a very positive outlook on life, and, although life had dealt her some nasty cards, she wasn't going to let things get her down.

Within six months of getting Lady, Stephanie had an operation to fuse her spine. When she came out of hospital, it was even harder to exercise Lady. Then something terrible happened. One day, while out walking, Lady broke off her lead and attacked another dog. Stephanie couldn't take any risks; with her disabilities, she had to have a dog she could control, so Lady was re-homed, much to everyone's distress. The family was beside itself with pain and loss. Stephanie knew she had to get another dog or her children wouldn't be able to cope. She also knew she had to have a dog who could be relied on one hundred per cent, which ruled out rescue dogs who might have problems. As a former social worker, she had access to information resources and rang three or four charities that provide support dogs for the disabled. None of them, however, worked in her local area of Southend-on-Sea. Then she came across an entry for the charity Canine Partners. To her delight, the charity operated nationwide and, unlike the other charities, was not limited to certain areas of the country. Stephanie rang Canine Partners, and within a few weeks one of its representatives visited her to see whether she might be a suitable partner for an assistance dog.

Unknown to Stephanie, a large chocolate Labrador named Frodo was wondering what exactly life had in store for him. Canine Partners had chosen Frodo from a breeder for training, but although he was extremely intelligent, he was also strong-willed and proving to be a handful with inexperienced people. 'We thought he was too pushy and he would sometimes bark at other dogs, or people,' admits Nina Bondarenko. 'So we gave him to the police to try out as a drug detection dog.'

Within two weeks, however, the police gave Frodo back.

His crime? He kept falling asleep while he was meant to be checking suspects on a line-up. To Nina's amazement, the police told her that he hadn't barked once at other dogs or people. Just as amazing, Frodo returned as a reformed character. He was, in fact, Mr Charm himself. 'I'm really sorry,' he seemed to say on getting back to the safety of Canine Partners. It was as if he was asking for another chance.

Slightly against her better judgement, Nina was tempted. This was no ordinary dog, she realised. What he needed was a partner as strong as him, in mental terms. Someone who could be on to him and wouldn't be scared of that huge brown bulk and boxer-like face. Someone, in fact, like Stephanie who had just contacted the charity. This was a woman who, despite an uncertain future, was not frightened of saying what she thought. It might just be worth giving it a go.

But Stephanie wasn't sure. Even though she hadn't met Frodo yet or even heard of him, she was beginning to have doubts about the whole undertaking. She had enjoyed her assessment day at Petersfield, where she had met several dogs and learned to give basic commands such as 'Heel', 'Sit down' and 'Stay'. But there was one big problem. She was very worried by Canine Partners' rule that their dogs shouldn't be stroked or fussed over by anyone else, apart from their partner, for six months. The rule is designed to build a strong bond between man or woman and dog – and it works well. But it's not easy to follow when everyone else in the family is yearning to give the dog a cuddle. 'I wanted a Canine Partner because I knew it would be well trained and would be able to help me lead a more independent life. But I knew the children would want to stroke and play with the dog.'

Stephanie rang Nina and told her about her worries. Nina pointed out that she couldn't relax the rule but advised Stephanie to think it over, which she did, for a whole month, talking about it relentlessly with her children. Eventually they decided that those six months wouldn't last for ever.

Difficult as it would be for them, they would try to abide by the rule because it was their only chance to have a dog who would be careful with their mother, who was now partly in a wheelchair, as well as with Emma, also partially wheelchair-bound, and Mark, who would soon need crutches.

So, with reservations, Stephanie enrolled on the Canine Partners 12-day residential training course. Like the other participants, she knew she would be tried out with different dogs and that she would not necessarily be given the first dog she was assigned during training. She also knew there was a possibility she wouldn't be given a dog at all if a suitable match wasn't found. There seemed to be a lot of uncertainties but Stephanie was used to that. She had discovered that life held no certainties, but by acknowledging that fact, she had learned to accept it.

Stephanie arrived at Canine Partners on a Sunday evening to begin her training course. Before meeting the dogs the following day, the group had a session on dog psychology to help them work more effectively with the different dogs they would be trying out over the next few days. They were taught to interpret the dog's feeling by observing the body language – for example, the tail held low could indicate uncertainty; and bright shining eyes with a raised wagging tail could indicate pleased confidence. Stephanie tried to remember these things, along with the more than ninety commands she and the rest of the group had been asked to memorise before the course began. When the dogs came into the training room on the Monday morning, she – like all the others on the course – was bowled over emotionally. All these dogs were lovely but seemed very lively as they checked everyone out, bouncing around, sniffing people in their wheelchairs, obviously thrilled to be finally off-lead and part of the action. When the dogs had eventually calmed down, Stephanie spotted a beautiful golden retriever called Flame. Now he, she thought to herself, would be absolutely perfect.

Somewhat taken aback, Stephanie was given the lead of a huge brown chocolate Labrador with an enormous crinkly face who looked a bit like Frank Bruno. 'I thought he was a great strong brute and I had some reservations. I didn't even like him, so how could I have him to live with me?' Like everyone else, however, Stephanie had been told to 'see how it went' with her 'blind date'. To her surprise, he did everything she told him on those first few days, acting like a gentle giant. The staff and Nina were amazed; Frodo had never behaved as well as this for anyone else. Yet Stephanie still couldn't feel much affection for him. Now, looking back, she can see why. 'I was holding back because of Lady. Having to give her away hurt so much that I didn't want to risk falling in love again in case I got hurt. I felt that if I acted aloof, I would protect myself.'

She hadn't taken Frodo's persistence into account. 'This woman might not feel anything for me at the moment,' he thought, 'but I'll get round her somehow. I'll be as good as gold and do everything she tells me so she can't help but fall for my charms.' He might have succeeded but, like many chaps, Frodo had one failing. He couldn't resist a pretty face, especially one particular face he used to know before he had met Stephanie. Towards the end of the first week, Stephanie was taking Frodo out for his afternoon walk along with everyone else in the group. As usual, Frodo was attached to her electric wheelchair and she was just beginning to think that maybe this dog wasn't so bad after all. Then disaster struck. Frodo spotted one of his old puppy parents, who now worked for Canine Partners. It was, for him, the equivalent of seeing his first love again. Without warning, he took off towards her, still attached to Stephanie's chair. It happened very quickly and she didn't have time to get the lead off. She was heading at speed towards the group (who had gone on ahead), and Frodo was totally focused on his former puppy-parent. Stephanie started to panic. She was wondering if she would end up in the pond that lay ahead, when Frodo suddenly skidded to a halt at the feet of his first love.

Many people in Stephanie's position would have got out and walked off, if they could. Trapped in her wheelchair, Stephanie wasn't able to do that. But instead of dissolving into tears, she was furious. 'You are never,' she shouted at Frodo, 'ever going to do that to me again. Do you understand?' Frodo himself did not seem particularly repentant. It took Stephanie and Frodo three times as long as the other dogs and their partners on the same exercise to walk back across the grounds to the building. All the way, Stephanie told Frodo off and made him walk to heel. The dog was not getting the better of her. And that was the end of it.

Although others had seen the incident, Stephanie found it difficult to discuss what had happened. She was upset and anxious. Only when she was back in her room, did she fully appreciate the great physical strength of these dogs. How could Nina even consider partnering her with such a dog? Nina herself came to see if Stephanie was all right. No, she told her, she wasn't. In fact, she thought she should go home, that she didn't love the dog, and that it wouldn't work out.

Nina is known for her uncanny knack at teaming up the right dogs with the right people. She told Stephanie that what had happened was an excellent lesson for any dog-handler and suggested that she shouldn't dismiss Frodo out of hand. 'Give it a few days,' she told her. 'Just think about it. You're the only person I've seen who has been able to bring out the best in that dog. He needs to learn to respect you and work with you.'

Although still doubtful, Stephanie agreed to stick with it, and to her amazement, Frodo was as good as gold for the rest of the course. He did so well that he graduated a day early, having passed all his tests with flying colours. It was as though Frodo had sown the last of his wild oats. He was now a changed dog and ready to settle down.

Stephanie was completely taken aback when Nina told her that she could go home with Frodo. After the last few days of perfect behaviour, she had begun to trust him again but she still wasn't completely certain. As she drove herself home in her automatic car, all kinds of doubts were flying round Stephanie's head. Supposing Frodo misbehaved, or even hurt Emma or Mark?

Yet deep down, she knew he was okay. The moment Frodo walked through the door of Stephanie's semi-detached home near Southend, it was as though he had been there before. 'He greeted the children like long-lost friends,' says Stephanie, 'and I'm afraid the six-month rule went out of the window. I rang Nina to say this is crazy. He's so friendly with them that I can't possibly stop them from touching him.'

Nina suggested a compromise. Rather than ignoring him completely and not touching him until he sat and shook hands, as they had been instructed to do, how about letting the children groom Frodo but only when Stephanie gave the command? That way, Frodo would know that Stephanie was the boss but the children could still be involved. It worked. Mark, Emma and James would ask for Stephanie's permission every time they touched him, a fact that did not go unnoticed by Frodo. Although he loved the children, Stephanie was still his number one. There was only one more problem to be resolved: how could he get Stephanie to reciprocate the feelings he had for her?

Determinedly, Frodo set about trying to win his mistress' heart. He not only did all the things he had been trained to do, such as pick up pens or keys that she dropped, he also used his initiative. Stephanie's dropped her crutch? Right, then he would pick it up for her even though it wasn't easy getting his nose round that awkward handle. The stairlift wasn't easy; when she got to the top, there was no room for him to get by because that big stairlift footplate was in the way. Still, he could do something about that, couldn't he? He'd simply push the footplate up with his nose and mouth so that he could get past and help her along the landing. Then there was that rather complicated manoeuvre when Stephanie was wheeling herself back to the car and needed to get her crutches out of the boot. He'd simply jump up and hand them to her; no need to be asked. Then, one day, Stephanie got into her stairlift at the top of the stairs and accidentally dropped one of her crutches. She was trapped because she couldn't get out without her crutches and yet couldn't go down on the stairlift because the crutch was in the way. In a flash, Frodo bounded down the stairs, extricated the crutch from under the lift shaft and brought it back to Stephanie so she could get downstairs.

First thing in the mornings, Frodo would help Steph get out of bed by pulling her up using a tug toy. 'I was amazed when I saw that Frodo was doing all these things on his own,' said Stephanie. 'I began to realise that he really loved me and that it was churlish to hold back because of Lady's memory. If you love someone, you have to accept the risks that go with it.'

Then, just as she began to relax, Frodo took a back step. He'd never been particularly keen on getting the washing out of the machine but on this particular day, he wasn't going to bother. Besides, there was so much of it! At the centre he had practised with only a few items, but in this household, there was always two or three loads a day. Really, it was too much for any dog. Stephanie repeated the command to get the washing out but Frodo still sat there, just looking at her. Right, she thought, two can play at that game. Canine Partners had taught her that she should never give a command more than twice. If she did, the dog would expect her to say it over and over again, before acting, rather like a naughty child. Instead, she should give him another command to get him back into the swing of doing what he was told. Going out into the garden, she told Frodo to sit, which he did, perfectly. Then she went back into the house and had a cup of tea, without talking to him. Stephanie knew that Frodo hated being ignored. Then she tried out the washing command again and this time Frodo did it.

The incident, however, stuck in Frodo's mind. For the next couple of months, he stubbornly refused to get out the washing on the first time of asking. Each time, Stephanie had to go through the charade of giving him another command, ignoring him and then asking him again. It reached the point where Stephanie began to wonder if it was really worth doing this at all. Then came the turning point. One day Stephanie was out in the local park with a friend and her partnership linker while Frodo was attached to her chair. Stephanie and her volunteer partnership linker, who makes regular visits to see how Stephanie and Frodo are getting on, were training Frodo not to go rushing up to say hello to other dogs until he was given a command. He is, after all, just a dog with an eye for a pretty (dog) face. He was being trained with an extending flexible lead, and as he ran forward to say hello, the lead slipped from Stephanie's hand and got trapped down the side of her wheelchair. Memories of that incident during the training course rushed back.

Stephanie was too slow at giving Frodo the command to stop and return to her, so he thought he was free to go. When he hit the end of the lead, he slipped sideways, tipping the chair over as he went, with Stephanie in it. Poor Frodo was beside himself with worry that Stephanie had been hurt. He fussed like an old mother hen, while Stephanie's partnership linker and her friend helped her up. They were there for insurance during the training, in case just such an incident happened. Stephanie was unhurt, and Frodo walked her home like an angel, constantly checking that she was okay. When she finally got home and slumped into her chair, Frodo settled himself on her feet, relieved that she was all right.

Concerned, Steph spoke to Nina who explained that amongst other things, there was still a battle of wills happening. Stephanie had got further with Frodo than anyone else had. If she wanted to give him back, Nina would understand completely. It was up to her. Stephanie looked at Frodo. During the last few weeks, he had tackled his reluctance to 'handle' the washing. So all right, he had chased after another dog but it was the first time and Stephanie was sure he wouldn't do it again. She would put this dog on probation; if he watched his step, he could stay. Besides, without being able to help it, she was beginning to feel deeply attached to this huge brown bear of a dog who obviously loved her so much.

Since this incident, over two years ago, Frodo hasn't been out of line once. If Stephanie wakes up feeling ill, he will know before anyone else. He almost seems to read her mind, and when she gives a command, is there before she has finished speaking. Stephanie's condition has continued to deteriorate and she now finds it hard to get up out of a chair or the bed. Frodo, however, he has learnt to take hold of a plastic tug while she holds the other end. His massive body weight – 38 kilos – then hauls her up. When she gets stuck while sitting down, he remembers the bracing lessons from the Canine Partners centre and will stand firm while she leans against him to get up. Talking of getting up, Stephanie doesn't suffer from the usual problems that mothers of teenagers have when their offspring are loath to get out of bed in the morning. All she has to do is say 'Go and get James' and Frodo will bound into James' room and lick him awake. Stephanie has recently taken on a part-time job at the Citizens Advice Bureau where, she says, people come to see Frodo as much as to see her. When she goes to work, Frodo carries a basket with all her essentials for the day.

Frodo also goes shopping with Stephanie; during a recent visit to the lingerie department, he accidentally knocked over an array of clothes. The assistant rushed to pick them up but Frodo got there first, handing her the clothes, still beautifully folded, in his mouth. 'How on earth does he do that?' asked the pretty shop assistant. Stephanie explained that Frodo's Canine Partners training taught him to pick things up very carefully with his teeth. It's done by clicker training; the command 'Pick up gently' is given and when a dog does this correctly, the trainer uses the clicker to make a noise and gives the dog a treat at the same time. If the dog simply rushes in, manhandling the object, there's no click and no treat.

Frodo not only provides physical support, he is also Stephanie's best friend and seems able to sense her thoughts and feelings. On bad days, when she finds it hard to get out of bed because of the pain, he likes to lie down on the floor or on the bed next to her, in sympathy. If she's feeling cold, he will bring her a blanket, often without being asked. And even when no one else is in the house, Stephanie never feels alone. How could she, with that adoring big brown face staring up at her lovingly?

About two and a half years after Frodo arrived, he was also subjected to the 'blind date' test. 'I'd decided I was fed up with being on my own,' explained Stephanie. 'But I was also aware that as a disabled mother of three, some men might not be interested. So I joined an internet dating agency.' For safety, Stephanie decided that she would leave Frodo in the car for the first meeting with each of her blind dates. If she took him with her, she was worried that the man might try to use Frodo to get to her or perhaps be more interested in the dog than in her. By leaving him in the car, she would be judged purely for herself; she also knew that if she ran into trouble and didn't come back, Frodo would raise the alarm. On the third date with a man, however, Stephanie took Frodo with her to see how he reacted. If he liked the man, she knew he would behave. But as we already know, it was only John who passed the 'Frodo' test.

Frodo welcomed John into the household with open paws; it was as though he knew John was a friend and not a threat. It's this kind of amazing intuition that has helped Frodo win a list of awards including Devotion to Duty Award by Pro Dogs in 1999, the Golden Bone Award from the Pet Role Trust in February 2000, The Working Pet award from Animal Planet 2001, and runner up in the BBC's Cleverest Animal in the World, 1999. He has also featured in several national newspaper articles and has even been voted 'Asda's Favourite Shopper'. As Stephanie explains, 'He loves to greet the staff when he goes shopping. Everyone looks out for him. I daren't go shopping without him, or else there is a cry of "Where's Frodo today?"' Frodo and Stephanie have also become celebrities in their village and are regularly called upon to give demonstrations for various groups. Recently, Frodo tried to 'save' his mistress from the lions at the zoo she visited with her granddaughter. 'The lioness began to knock on the glass when she saw Frodo and he thought she was trying to attack me. So he jumped up on my lap to protect me, and kept barking until the lioness backed off. It's a long way from that inauspicious start just three years ago.

'It just goes to show,' says Stephanie as she strokes Frodo's head lovingly, 'that love doesn't always happen at first sight. I don't know how I would manage without him; I love him to bits. He is always with me, and is even happier now that I have someone who loves me as much as he does. He always lies between John and me, so he is touching both of us, just like a triangle. His love match is complete.'

ECHO *and* ENID

Echo and Enid were staying the night in a hotel for a work conference when the fire alarm went off. Knowing that fire alarms often go off by accident in hotels, 62-year-old Enid turned over and tried to go back to sleep. But Echo, a large black cross between an Irish water-spaniel and a golden retriever, wasn't happy. Pulling back Enid's sheet, he put his cold nose on her shoulder as though to say, 'Come on, you've got to do something.' Reluctantly Enid opened the door and looked down the empty corridor. Everyone else was probably asleep, just as she should be. But Echo gave a short sharp bark and looked at Enid worriedly. 'All right,' she said. 'Have it your way. We'll just go and have a look. But let me get my dressing gown first.' Just at that moment, friends from the conference banged on the door. 'There's a fire,' they yelled. 'Come on, we've got to go outside.'

Enid, Echo and the other guests were ushered outside to the courtyard by staff, where they stood, shivering in their white hotel dressing gowns, waiting for the fire brigade to arrive. The fire, which had started in staff quarters, was not big but it took nearly half an hour before firemen pronounced the building safe enough for them to go back inside. No one had been injured but Enid was acutely aware that it could have been more serious and that if she had ignored Echo's warning, she could have been hurt. 'Echo had sensed the danger just like the dogs who rescued their owners in America on 11 September,' said Enid proudly.

Enid believes that Echo is a gift from God. Every day, as they walk through the woods near their home in Wiltshire, they often sing, with Echo making the occasional sound in accompaniment. 'The woods are our cathedral,' says Enid as she fondly strokes Echo's black curly coat. 'We come here to think and pray as we walk along.'

But Enid hasn't always seen Echo this way. When she first spoke to Canine Partners about the possibility of getting a dog, she made one thing plain. She had to have a golden retriever, definitely not a black dog because some years earlier, a black collie had bitten one of her children. Also, Enid's eldest daughter, Jayne, is registered blind and Enid thought she might have trouble spotting a black dog when she came to stay. Sure enough, when Enid visited Canine Partners for an initial assessment day, she spotted a beautiful golden retriever who exactly fitted the picture she had in her mind. But at the same time, she couldn't help noticing a large black, curly-haired dog, lying against the wall with a doleful expression on his face. Echo looked utterly fed up and Enid's heart went out to him. He looked so miserable that she couldn't help going up and stroking him. 'It's all right,' she reassured him. 'I'm sure someone will want you one day.'

What Enid didn't know was that Echo's hang-dog expression is not always to be taken seriously. He might look fed up, but Enid is now convinced that Echo was an actor in a former life because he's so good at playing up to an audience. He is also dashingly good-looking. Echo is the first Canine Partners crossbreed. His mother, a stunning Irish

79

water-spaniel appeared to have finished her season and was left by her breeder in the same room as a golden retriever. The result was a litter of nine puppies, five of whom were sadly put down because the breeder thought he wouldn't be able to find homes for them. Nina tested the remaining four but only Echo passed her tests. She could tell that despite that spaniel eagerness, which made him rush in a little too fast, he had the intelligence to make a good dog. 'He was like the child at school,' says Nina, 'who's always first to put up his hand but doesn't know the answer when he's finally picked. But there was also something about this little tangle of black hair with those bright eyes peeping out, that made me think this could be something...'

Echo was also a stunning puppy, taking after his mother's almost gypsy-like Irish beauty instead of his father's golden genes. The spaniel legacy has resulted in long, floppy ears, which Echo shakes around with great effect. But in spite of his good looks, Echo is a gift that Enid would have turned down were it not for her four grown-up children, Jayne, Rory, Sarah and Geoffrey. Enid had brought all four up on her own after her husband had left them when Geoffrey was only 16 months old. Determined to cope and, at this stage, in good health, she took a job as a housekeeper/cook because the post came with a house. It also allowed her to make sure the children got off to school and back. By the time she was in her early forties, however, Enid began to feel unwell. Her left thumb went numb, which may have been explained by the fact that she had burned it; but it didn't explain the pins and needles in her leg. Her doctor, presuming that Enid was worrying unnecessarily, reluctantly sent her to a neurologist who declared her fit. At 42, Enid went back to the surgery and saw a different doctor. On the Tuesday of the following week, she was at the neurologist once more. And by Thursday, she was diagnosed with multiple sclerosis and pernicious anaemia, which had caused irreparable damage to her spine.

It was, says Enid, a relief rather than a bombshell. She had felt ill for so long but, in the light of the earlier doctor's prognosis, had begun to wonder if she was being neurotic. Now at least she had got to the root of the problem. With the help of the local council, Enid gave up work and eventually moved into an adapted home that was on one level. By now, she was relying increasingly on her walking frame and an electric wheelchair outside the home. But her children were still worried. All four had now left home, and Sarah was living in California with her American husband. Although they phoned and visited regularly, they were apprehensive in case their mother fell and there was no one to help. They were also concerned that she would be lonely. Although Enid is a sociable, chatty person who is heavily involved with local organisations and committees, it isn't the same as living with someone.

Then Enid read about assistance dogs in her *MS* magazine. It seemed a good idea but it wasn't for her. Three years earlier, Enid had had an English springer spaniel cross called Brontë after the author Emily. Brontë had lived to a ripe age and Enid couldn't consider replacing her. Her daughter Jayne thought otherwise. She, too, read the article and thought that a Canine Partner was exactly what her mother needed. The family encouraged Enid to contact Canine Partners for one of their dogs and the application forms were duly despatched.

Somewhat reluctantly, Enid agreed to find out a bit more, if only to keep her children happy. A Canine Partners assessor came round to her home to check it was suitable and that Enid herself was capable of taking on the big commitment of owning a dog. She was then invited on a one-day assessment, which is where she found Echo, languishing in a corner and eyeing everyone mournfully. 'I was given two or three dogs to work with that day and one was Echo. It certainly wasn't love at first sight but at the same time, I was intrigued. Echo seemed very subdued and moody, rather like a difficult artist. But when he got excited about something, he'd become really lively. Then he'd lapse back into his contemplative mood again. He was a real mystery, like a person who is hiding his real feelings.'

After completing the assessment, Enid was then asked to come back on a 12-day course in the summer. However, she was unable to make the dates; although Enid doesn't have a full-time paid job, she has numerous voluntary activities, which take up much of her time. Although she didn't know it then, Enid was running a risk. Echo, who was due to be on that course, could easily have been partnered with someone else. But Nina's intuition told her that Echo was worth holding back until Enid could attend the next course. It was a gamble because it may be that they wouldn't work out. However, it was a gamble Nina was prepared to take.

Yet would it work out? Nina was soon to find out when Enid went on the next Canine Partners course in October, along with two other hopeful recipients, Bernie and Jenny, who are also wheelchair users. Enid will never forget that first morning when, as the three women waited expectantly, a Canine Partners helper came into the room with three dogs on leads.

'Oh good, there's Feargal,' said Bernie who was excited to see the dog she had met before.

'Fantastic, there's Free,' said Jenny who had also fallen in love with this chocolate Labrador on the previous assessment days.

'Good heavens,' said Enid surprised. 'I've got Echo. And what on earth have you done to him?'

Poor Echo had had a severe haircut and, if it weren't for the doleful expression and floppy ears, Enid might not even have recognised him. 'I thought he would have been placed by then but I heard, unofficially, that Nina had thought we would suit each other so had held him back until I came on the course. I'm so glad that she did! It also turned out that Echo was Feargal's half-brother because they shared the same father.'

But at the time, Enid wondered if she could really love this dog with the long face. She also hated being in residential accommodation; being an independent woman, to her it felt like an institution. The course was exhausting too. Physically, it was hard work learning to make the dogs follow the commands, which they had been asked to learn before the course began. In addition to these stresses, Enid's physical illness caused her to tire very easily. At times, she broke down and cried, sometimes in front of the trainers. The final straw was that Echo didn't always do as he was told. One day, he shot off into the rosemary bushes and wouldn't come out. Enid felt like going home. Echo, however, had other ideas.

Towards the end of that first week, they did another off-lead exercise during which the dogs are meant to walk close to the wheelchairs without their leads on. Suddenly, without warning, Echo came up to Enid and placed his head on her knee as though to say 'You know, I really do love you.' Enid burst into tears; for her it was a turning point. If this dog needed her that badly, she couldn't turn him down. But now she had to prove that she could manage him. Echo was a strong-willed character, clever but not subservient. If he wanted to do something, that was fine. If not, Enid had to use all her negotiating skills to persuade him. During the second week of the course, it rained fiercely. Echo took a dislike to the lift at the back of the minibus, which hoisted the wheelchairs in and out. To encourage him to ignore the noise, Enid (feeling like a naughty schoolgirl) saved sausages from breakfast to give him as treats. The other women did the same to reward their dogs during the daily exercises. It wasn't strictly encouraged but they were desperate. They hoped to make their dogs respond more quickly.

This wasn't easy. Each dog had already been taught to respond to a specific word or phrase, which would, in turn, prompt the dog to do a particular task. Enid, like all the others, had to learn these words; but if she got one wrong or out of sequence, the dog wouldn't respond. It was like trying to remember nearly a hundred verbal pin codes. To make things even more difficult, Enid's MS meant she often mixed words up or said words she didn't mean to say. During one of the tests in the second week, the women had to sit at a restaurant table while their dogs went underneath. The command was 'Down' but Enid came out with 'Settle down'. The latter command means the dog can sit where he wants, but forgetting this, Enid couldn't understand why Echo wasn't sitting still under her table. It wasn't until a trainer called out 'Down' that she realised why.

It's a big challenge to make 'your' dog do what you say when it is also in contact with trainers who have been teaching it for the past two years. Suddenly, the dog has to learn to obey a person it has known for only ten days.

Another text was the 'Down, stay' command when the dog has to stay in the same position while its partner goes off for three minutes. 'We all hid behind a phone box,' recalls Enid, 'but to my horror, a man patted Echo, looking around for his owner. I was sure that Echo was going to get up and walk off with him. But he didn't. I can't describe how proud and happy I felt when the three minutes were up and I wheeled myself up to him to find he hadn't twitched a muscle!'

The three women celebrated their survival on the bus going home with a bag of cheese straws they had bought from the bakers. 'We felt really close; we were all in this together. But we couldn't help worrying in case one of us didn't make it.' They needn't have worried. That night Nina asked them what they wanted to do the following day. They all looked at each other in confusion. 'We thought we had to do our test,' they said. 'Why bother,' asked Nina, 'when you've done so well today?'

All three women were over the moon. Finally they could go home with their dogs. But unlike her new friend Bernie, who had a family to go back to, Enid was taking Echo back to her empty bungalow. Would a woman who had been on her own for so many years get used to living with someone else again? In fact, it was her saving grace. 'Until Echo arrived, my days stretched out before me without a pattern. There was no need to cook myself a proper meal or even go out of the house. I wasn't a recluse but I didn't have much of a purpose to my day. My children had gone and I was an empty-nester.'

But Echo soon filled that nest. Having a dog in the house meant Enid had to establish a routine just as she had done when the children had been at home. Echo needed walking, before lunch and afterwards. He also had to be fed so she made herself a proper meal at the same time, talking to him as she prepared it. Very soon, Enid learned to lean on Echo – literally. Because of his height and size (he weighs 35.6 kilos), she was able to rest on him when her legs felt weak and she needed support before reaching for her frame or wheelchair.

Echo also accompanied Enid to her voluntary committee meetings and occasional conferences. It was during one of these, held at a hotel in the New Forest, that Echo alerted her to the blaze. 'From that minute on, I've always listened to Echo when he tries to tell me something. He always barks if someone comes into our cul-de-sac and I take notice if he doesn't like someone. A dog is a very good judge of character – often more so than humans.' As a member of a housing committee, Enid frequently has meetings in a big boardroom at the local authority offices. Echo sits quietly beneath the table and will then go out to lunch with everyone after- wards. He also sits with Enid at disability tribunals when plaintiffs appeal against the amount of money they have been awarded to help with their impairment. 'People are often surprised to see me in a wheelchair and Echo with his identity jacket on,' says Enid. 'It helps to break the ice. It's a difficult time for them; they have come to ask for more money and they feel nervous. But a dog introduces a note of normality into an otherwise formal occasion. Afterwards, they often come up and ask if they can pat him.'

Recently Enid and Echo appeared on local radio. The studio was hardly big enough for Echo to sit down and Enid was worried when the producer asked if she could demon- strate the things that Echo could do. How could she when the audience could only hear instead of see? But the producer said not to worry; he would describe what Enid was doing. It wasn't easy in such a limited space but somehow Enid managed to drop keys, which Echo would pick up perplexedly. 'What on earth are we doing this for?' he seemed to ask.

Once a week, during fine weather, Enid and Echo walk the five miles to Marlborough, Enid in her chair and Echo attached on his lead. Echo's favourite shop is Waitrose where he is known at the cheese counter and rewarded with a free taster of Cheddar. Enid is used to everyone smiling at her as she does her shopping, but one day she realised they were smiling more than usual. Looking around, she saw that Echo had half a French loaf in his mouth. Apparently a child had dropped it and Echo had picked it up, just as he did at home. He hadn't eaten a mouthful (even though he's very partial to a baguette) but simply thought he was doing what Enid wanted. He can't, however, resist a carrot and one day, having carried a bag of carrots home, helped himself when alone in the kitchen.

To clean up after their walks, Enid takes Echo into the shower with her, which he loves. Afterwards, he tears around the house as Enid tries to dry him with his own flannelette sheets and towels. That's another of Echo's little quirks; he loves ripping sheets, but providing they're his own, it doesn't matter too much. He also loves ripping wrapping paper, and on Christmas Day he undoes his own presents. Last year he had a little toy dog, wearing a red coat, which makes noises.

Enid also likes to take Echo to the Mobility Road Show at Crowthorne in Berkshire where they help at the Canine Partners stand. One year, a woman came up to her. 'I've been watching you,' she said, 'and I just had to say that you and your dog are like a ballet. Everywhere you go he follows. It's like synchronised dancing.' Echo isn't just on Enid's wavelength either; he is very astute at picking up vibes from other people. He regularly goes to church with Enid and accompanies her to a Christian retreat twice a year. Once, during a healing service, he was unable to settle as usual below the pew. 'What's wrong?' asked one of the wardens but Enid wasn't sure. He finally settled down when she took him to the back of the church, away from the rows of people in front who had all come for healing. Later, after the service had finished, she took him back to the church and he behaved normally. Enid is convinced that Echo had picked up on someone's pain, which physically hurt him too. He certainly knows when she herself is in pain from her MS. 'He'll stay by my side, very quietly, as though he knows I don't want him to fuss. But if I want something, he'll bring it to me often before I even ask him. The other day, he brought my cardigan in from the bedroom because I was cold.'

This is another amazing thing about a Canine Partner. Enid doesn't remember shivering with cold or even telling Echo that she was feeling the chill. He just seemed to sense that this was the case. That kind of unspoken intuition between dog and partner is exactly what makes these partnerships so special and different. You can train a dog to do all kinds of extraordinary things but it's that deep understanding of each other's needs, hopes and fears that is so unique.

Just as crucial is a Canine Partner's ability to learn on the job. Intuition isn't something that can be taught in puppy classes. It's either there at the beginning or it isn't. If it is there, it can be nurtured, as Enid and Echo have shown. The longer they live with each other, the more in tune they are.

In the evening, Echo loves being read to; he prefers poetry or even excerpts from a novel. Enid is a keen reader and Echo always goes with her to the mobile library, which comes every other Tuesday. Sometimes Enid reads her paperwork aloud and Echo makes no pretence at hiding his boredom. He'll put his head down on the ground, between his paws, and sigh heavily. Echo is a master at sighing, but like some humans, he often does it out of habit. It doesn't always mean he's fed up. At night, Echo has a bed in Enid's room. Often he wakes when it's pitch black and wanders into the sitting room to gather his thoughts. But before he does, he always stretches up on Enid's side of the bed and puts his cold nose on her hands, to warn her that he's off and will be back soon.

Enid has now had Echo for nearly three years but Canine Partners is always there to offer help if she needs it. When Echo cut his paw on a bottle in the woods and had to have clips (like stitches), she rang to tell Canine Partners what was happening and get reassurance. Like all Canine Partners recipients, Enid submits a six-monthly report to tell the charity how Echo is doing, and once a year, Alison Keeling, the after-care officer, pays a friendly visit. Enid looks forward to the annual Canine Partners summer barbecue when many of the dogs and their partners are reunited. 'There's a wonderful pond and all the dogs so swimming. Some of them seem to recognise each other but the amazing thing is that there are never any fights.' A wonderful acknowledgement came for Echo in February 2002 when he was awarded 'Support Dog of the Year' at the Golden Bone Awards, given by the Pet Role Trust.

Enid is determined that Echo will never be forgotten. During the millennium celebrations, her village put together a capsule of items and memories from 1999. Enid was asked to write a description of Echo and what he has done for her, as well as put in a photograph. The capsule will be opened in the year 2200, and Enid wishes she could be around to see what people think of him. Meanwhile, what does the future hold for her? Enid glances across the room to where Echo is lying by the back door, watching for squirrels. As if he knows she is looking at him, he turns and cocks his head on one side. 'I'd like to think we'll grow old disgracefully together.' Echo gives a big sigh. 'Sounds good to me,' he seems to say.

IKON *and* JOHN

It's one o'clock on a Wednesday morning in the office. Ikon sits up, stretches out on his sheepskin mat, yawns and emerges from his space under the computer desk. It's coffee time and, like most office workers, Ikon doesn't need reminding. Besides, the coffee bar next door is one of his favourite places. Where else can a dog get a drink and a cuddle from his workmates at the same time?

Not all Canine Partners go to work with their owners but this lovely yellow Labrador is an exception. Since he was partnered with 45-year-old John Gunn, a computer analyst from Aylesbury, in the summer of 2000, Ikon has been invaluable round the office. John is severely arthritic and has been in a wheelchair from the age of five. Although he is able to write with a pen and hold a phone, he often drops them on the floor. Before Ikon arrived, someone else had to pick them up, which was both frustrating for John and time-consuming for other people in the office. Now Ikon does it for him. He will also open the office door, pick up keys and, at the end of the day, hold John's wheelchair steady in the car park as he heaves himself into his adapted BMW to drive home.

As well as this, Ikon provides light-relief in John's office, which is based in Aylesbury at Manor House Hospital, for patients with learning difficulties. When John and Ikon walk down the corridor towards the coffee bar for that mid-morning break, patients stop to admire his beautiful pale gold coat. Many of these patients cannot talk or walk but their eyes light up when they see Ikon. He also helps break the ice for John, a shy quietly spoken Glaswegian who has been through more than most of us could ever imagine.

John's story starts back in 1958 when, at the age of three, he inexplicably developed severe juvenile arthritis. He doesn't remember much about his life before his illness, although, poignantly, he can dimly recall riding a bicycle. After that, his memories blur into a never-ending cycle of pain, hospitals and lying in bed, finding it hard to move. By the time he was five, he was in a wheelchair and his parents had separated. Unable to cope, John's mother had sent him to a convalescent home until he was eight and then to a residential school for the physically disabled in Edinburgh. Although he went home for school holidays, John preferred the stability of school. John hadn't grown up in a dog-loving family but, to his delight, many of the staff at school owned dogs. His favourite was a black Labrador whom he used to stroke and talk to. There was, John discovered, something very special in confiding in someone whose deep brown eyes suggested he understood exactly what this small boy was going through even if he couldn't talk back.

But at 17, John realised he had to make a choice. Either he could go on living in residential care or he could try to forge an independent life for himself. Determined to do the latter, he took a college course in electronics and administration while living with his mother. It wasn't easy going home again; school had given him an education and positive attitude, which meant he had little in common with his family. 'I also missed having a dog around and decided that I would try to get a place of my own so I could have one.'

After college, John got a job with the civil service and had his name down for a council flat. But fate had other plans. In 1979, when he was 21, John suffered severe kidney failure and was on a dialysis machine for two years. His only chance of survival was to have a transplant, but donors were few and far between. However, one soon became available and the operation was a success. Although John was still in a wheelchair, he had been given a new lease of life. Finally, he was able to move into a home of his own in Glasgow, provided by the council. John's first step was to find that dog he'd always wanted.

'I didn't want a puppy because I knew I'd find one hard to train in my position. So I scoured the local papers and found an advert for an eight-month-old German shepherd who was being sold by a nearby farmer. I liked the shape of his head and the way he looked at me. Even though I was in a chair, I felt sure I could look after him.' Rocky was exactly what John needed. Although he was a pet – John hadn't heard of Canine Partners at this stage – he was someone to talk to. By this time, John had a job in the local council housing department as an administrative worker. But, it wasn't easy living on his own. 'Boarding school hadn't taught me to be very streetwise. I found it hard to cope with simple things like paying bills and cooking and shopping.'

To John's credit, however, he continued to battle on, despite having to have two knee operations, a hip operation and another kidney transplant. Apart from Rocky, the other great love of his life was wheelchair table tennis and rugby, which he had started at school. Little did he know that ultimately this would lead him to his future partner and also to Ikon. John started to compete in both basketball at national level and wheelchair rugby at national and international level. In 1989, he went to the wheelchair games at Stoke Mandeville in Buckinghamshire where he met his partner, Jennifer, who was one of the nurses covering the games. It wasn't, he says, love at first sight but they both had a good sense of humour and enjoyed each other's company. After he went home, John began to drive down to see Jennifer at weekends, and within a year, he moved to Buckinghamshire to be with her.

At last it seemed that John had a chance of living a normal life. The pair set up home near the hospital, and after a few months John found a job as a wheelchair sales rep and also joined a local pressure group committee to fight for better facilities for the disabled. Then in 1999, Rocky died, aged thirteen and a half, and John was devastated. 'I know he'd had a full life but I missed him dreadfully. Jennifer works shifts so is out a lot; there was a big hole without Rocky.'

At the back of his mind, John remembered Canine Partners, a charity he had come across at Crufts a few years ago while visiting the show. He'd been very interested in the Canine Partners stall and their demonstration dogs who were able to help special-needs owners by picking up things and opening doors and finding keys. John had come away from the stall with an application form and an information leaflet, which he had filed away in case he needed it one day. Now, after Rocky's death, he remembered them. But it was too soon to think about replacing his beloved pet. John is a quiet, thoughtful man whose many years in a wheelchair have taught him to be patient and take his time. So he waited for nearly 12 months before filling in the forms.

'I knew I was getting older and needed help,' admits John. 'There'd been quite a few occasions when Jennifer had been out and I'd dropped the phone at home and not been able to reach it. I didn't feel I'd reached the stage where I needed a full-time carer but it would definitely be helpful to have an extra hand. And because I loved dogs, Canine Partners seemed the perfect solution.'

But it wasn't as easy as that. The careful administration of the assessment procedure meant it took nearly three months before Canine Partners made a routine visit to see how suitable John's home was for a dog, and whether he himself seemed an appropriate owner. On the surface, he appeared a good candidate, partly because he'd already been a dog-owner and also because his bungalow has a garden with fields at the bottom where he can 'walk' in his electric chair. Nevertheless, John was apprehensive. He desperately wanted to be accepted on the Canine Partners course but, as he'd been warned, there were no guarantees. Competition was fierce; about three-quarters of Canine Partners applicants are turned down, usually because they don't have the right home environment or because they are unable to cope with the responsibility of a dog. Even if John was accepted, he knew he would have to be teamed with the right dog. If there wasn't one available, he might have to wait months or even years.

Five weeks later, John received the phone call he'd been waiting for. He was invited to go to Hampshire for the day to assess how he reacted with different dogs. Jennifer drove him down; although she hadn't grown up with dogs, she had loved Rocky and could see the benefits of having another dog who was also specially trained to help people with extra needs. John was teamed up with a variety of dogs during the day. Canine Partners name their dogs in batches, under each letter of the alphabet, and at that time, they were coming to the end of their *G* group of dogs so John had Geordie, a black Labrador. All the dogs seemed wonderful to John but he knew he was unlikely to be teamed up immediately. Nina had already explained that everyone would be tried out with a variety of dogs over the next few weeks. The *I* group, to which Ikon was to belong, hadn't yet come through; John didn't know it, but his future dog was still living with his puppy parent, Di Currie, before going to Canine Partners for four months of more intensive training.

During the day, John and the four others in his group were taught simple commands such as 'Come here' and 'Heel'. They were also shown how to use high-pitched voice commands to attract the dogs' attention. 'I felt increasingly excited as I realised how much a Canine Partner would be able to help me,' says John. 'But I also thought it was a really big commitment.'

John enjoyed his day and was invited to come back to the centre the following month for another session where he met Finian, a chocolate Labrador. John liked him but was told he barked a lot; he later found out Finian was taken out of the programme because of this. He also met another dog called Igor who seemed a possible match but was later withdrawn because of arthritic problems. John's visits to find his perfect match continued for a further nine months. A less patient person might have found this frustrating but John was content to wait. Having met Nina Bondarenko, he had faith in her; she would know when the right dog came along for him.

Then, in August 2000, he was invited on a 12-day residential course, which meant that Canine Partners thought they might have found the right dog for him. John, a naturally cautious man, couldn't help feeling excited. Was it, he wondered, Ivory, one of the yellow Labradors he'd worked with during the last couple of sessions? Canine Partners does not tell a potential recipient that he or she has been definitely teamed up with a certain dog in case it doesn't work out. Instead, John's group of five (which included David Beard and Ian Free) were warned when they arrived on that Sunday evening that they would be tried out with one four-legged partner but that they may well be swapped around during the course. It was a bit like going out with four other couples and preparing yourself for the possibility of going home with someone else's date.

Again, according to Canine Partners practice, John's group didn't meet the dogs until the following morning. As they waited, the dogs were suddenly released into the training room and ran around, wild with excitement. John and the others all laughed with surprise; any reservations they had about getting to know each other as a group were immediately dispelled by this band of licky affectionate puppies who couldn't wait to get started. John was pleased to see Ivory and suspected he was meant for him. On the other hand, life had taught him not to set his heart on anything. Nina knew what she was doing; he would be guided by her.

Slightly to his surprise, John was partnered with Ikon that morning, although he knew this might change. Like his brother Ivory, Ikon had a beautiful pale gold coat, and John had always secretly yearned for a dog this colour. John is too reserved a man to allow himself to fall instantly in love with his dog, as some of the other Canine Partners recipients have done. He was also different from other members of his group because he had been ill all his life and had not suddenly been disabled because of an accident. This made John naturally cautious; Ikon seemed nice but he wouldn't allow himself to get too attached in case they didn't work out. And he certainly couldn't see the bond between them that everyone else could.

In fact, John and Ikon appeared to be complete opposites. Here was this dog who loved showing off and would swagger into the room, like a movie star, just as his brother did. 'Hey, look at me,' he would seem to be saying. In contrast, John preferred to stay in the background, quietly getting on with his life. Still, they say that opposites attract, and Nina certainly hoped this was the case. She had spotted something special about Ikon on the day she had tested him along with his brother Ivory. Like many Canine Partners dogs, Ikon and Ivory had come to her attention through a breeder's advert in *Dogs Today*. Good dogs are hard to come by; out of every 50 dogs tested, Canine Partners might choose only two, so Nina was always on the look-out for potential candidates. This particular breeder lived in Manchester and was, according to Nina, slightly overwhelmed; this was the breeder's first litter and she hadn't realised how lively small puppies could be. Ikon and Ivory were particularly bouncy and ran up to greet Nina in the small hallway. She tested all six puppies in the litter to see how sociable they were and how willing they were to retrieve. 'Assistance dogs are much more difficult to find than show dogs because they have to do more. A show dog simply has to come out of a car, walk around a ring and then get back into the car. The kind of dogs we need have to be fit, physically brave and bursting with initiative and sociability.' Ivory and Ikon were the only pair in the litter to pass Nina's tests, but even so, she had some misgivings. They were almost too confident, rather like a pair of terrible twins.

Both puppies were around six weeks old, an ideal age, because they shouldn't have picked up bad habits. As with most Canine Partners puppies, the pair went straight to their puppy parents who had already been chosen and were waiting. Ikon's new home was with Di Currie, a mother of three teenagers from Haslemere in Surrey who had already fostered two previous Canine Partners puppies. Di remembers Ikon as quite a character. 'He swaggered confidently like a little warthog; yet, for the first month, he howled at night for attention until he was finally banished to the boiler room where no one could hear him.' He also had a soft spot for the laundry basket where he was once found, fast asleep, in the garden by the washing line. 'He loved charging around with other dogs and once ran straight into a brick wall,' says Di. 'He just shook his head and carried on running – a real old toughie! His favourite trick was to pull off other dogs' collars at Canine Partners training classes. But he didn't manage to do this with my own old retriever, Willow, who only just tolerated him.'

This stage of a Canine Partners's life is meant to include a certain amount of fun; it's a gentle transition stage before going on to real work. So after a puppy has been with his family for between nine and 14 months, it will then go into Canine Partners kennels for intensive training. This might take between three and six months, depending on the dog.

This intensive training includes more complicated tasks such as taking off people's jackets or putting on socks. Nina uses her own special errorless learning technique, based on rewarding a puppy for the right kind of behaviour and ignoring the wrong response. The rewards vary according to what the dog likes best; it might be food or it might be the opportunity to say hello to another dog or it might be a quick rest. Whatever form the reward takes, it acts as a trigger so that the dog learns to do the 'right thing' to get the treat.

Ikon had finished his intensive training shortly before he met John. Now Nina was hoping all her hard work would pay off and that this might be the match she'd been waiting for. 'It wasn't easy. John was very withdrawn and his shyness came across as difficult behaviour at first. Ikon, in contrast, was dancing around, demanding that everyone should look at him. But when he was with John, I could see that there was something going on there; a definite rapport.'

Perhaps because he was too scared to let himself go, John himself couldn't see this bond. Instead, he concentrated hard on working with Ikon during this very intensive 12-day training course. They learned to do practical things such as how to get in a shopping centre lift. First the dog has to sit. On command, he then jumps up and presses the Call button. When the lift arrives, it's important to push the chair over the threshold so that the doors stay open for the dog, who will come into the lift from behind. When getting out, it's chair over the threshold with the dog behind and then the dog goes forward. The procedure may sound unnecessarily detailed but it is vital to ensure that both dog and owner get in and out safely.

John and the rest of the group also learned how to cross the road. Never stand at the edge because the length of lead could allow the dog to wander out. And always keep yourself between the traffic and the dog because a motorist will spot a pedestrian before an animal. There is a mock shop in the training room with plastic bottles containing different weights on shelves. John learned the command 'Look, look' and watched as Ikon picked up a bottle. If it was the wrong one, he'd say 'Wrong' and when Ikon picked up the right one, he would say 'Get it!' in a very high excited voice. Voice control is crucial with all these exercises. John and the others were taught to speak in high-pitched tones, which is difficult for men. There were, says John lots of giggles over this, which, according to John, helped to bond the group and their dogs together. 'Ikon was very intelligent but he was also extremely excitable and almost crazy,' said John. 'Once, when he picked up my expensive sunglasses for me, he was so enthusiastic that he broke them. At times I thought I wouldn't be able to cope. But Ivory and Ikon were very verbal and "talked" a lot during the exercises. It made me realise this was just as strange for him as it was for me.'

At the end of each day, the dogs slept in their partners' rooms. Ikon had been specially taught by Canine Partners to take John's socks on and off, something John found difficult with his limited hand movement. Little things like this might seem insignificant to those of us who can do them without thinking; but to John, it was one less arduous job to be done. When he woke up in the morning, Ikon was already up, breezily wagging his tail and ready to go. Faced with such enthusiasm, John had to make sure he performed his part of the bargain by doing everything he had been taught.

At the end of the 12-day residential course came the final test that every dog and partner has to pass before they can be formally paired. In preparation, they did a mock test, rather like the one L-drivers take, to see if they were ready for the real thing. Even though it was a practice, the experience was nerve-wracking. The group had to make an ambitious shopping trip round Horsham, visiting several shops and going in and out of lifts. Trainers were positioned at different spots to see how they got on. John knew that he and Ikon had the lift technique down to a fine art. They were also good at crossing roads. But the one exercise he was dreading, was the 'Down, stay' when the dog is told to lie down and wait while his handler disappears out of sight. John's instructions were to leave Ikon in a busy part of a shopping mall for between one to two minutes. It was a big test for an intelligent dog who was dying to explore what was going on around him. Although John couldn't see this, while he was hiding a small girl came up and patted Ikon. If Ikon had got up in response, he would have failed the course, which would have meant John and Ikon would not have been partnered. But he didn't. 'I was so proud when the trainer told me this,' said John. 'I really felt he'd been trying as hard as I had.' The group also had to sit a written test – A typical question: if there is a narrow aisle in the shop, what is the best way to manage the situation? One answer might be to have the dog work behind the wheelchair.

At the end of the day, the group was given a choice. They could either go for the results of that day's dry-run test, which they didn't know yet, or, if they felt they could do better, do the real thing the next day. John felt that he and Ikon had done a pretty good job so he chose to accept the result of the mock test. So, too, did the rest of the group. Only then were they given the results. They had all passed. John gave Ikon a big hug and the dog grinned from ear to ear as if he knew what he had achieved. Each couple was then allowed to take a walk round the grounds without a trainer; until then, a trainer had always accompanied them. It was like taking a new baby out for the first time; a huge responsibility but also a wonderful achievement. During the walk, John talked quietly to Ikon, praising him and telling him about the new home he was taking him to and the wonderful future they would have together. For a man who had never permitted himself to show much feeling, this was as big a turning point in John's life as it was in Ikon's.

To celebrate, the group went out for a meal and a couple of glasses of wine while the dogs sat quietly under the table. Ikon behaved himself beautifully. 'You see,' he tried to say. 'I can perform when I want but I also understand the art of resting between performances.'

But how would Ikon cope with going home with John, and would Ikon and Jennifer bond as well as he and John had? To be truthful, both John and Jennifer, who came to collect him, were a little nervous, but there was no cause for worry. Ikon immediately slotted into John's way of life and enjoyed his long walks across the fields behind the house. Meanwhile, John asked his bosses if it was possible to bring him into the office where he works a 15-hour week. 'I was a bit worried about it because I knew Ikon was very enthusiastic even though he was calming down. I didn't want him knocking anyone over in the corridor.' However, as soon as Ikon went into the building and saw there were several other people in wheelchairs, he seemed to go very quiet. It was as if he knew he had to be careful. He's also aware of John's health. At present, John is waiting for another hip replacement operation; and over the years, his bones have become soft and easy to break. This makes it even more difficult for John to try to bend down to get something so Ikon is always on the alert. There are, however, temptations in the office. If someone opens a packet of crisps, it's very hard for a dog not to help pick up the crumbs. And it's not surprising that every now and then, all that attention from staff and patients goes to his head. 'Yes,' he seems to say as yet another person stops to admire him. 'I really am quite a handsome chap, aren't I?'

But as well as being an office dog, Ikon has another role. For two days a week, John works in Birmingham, coaching the Birmingham Bandits, a wheelchair rugby team. Ikon goes along, travelling in a dog-crate in the back of John's car. Inside the sports hall, he lies at the side and watches the ball carefully. And as soon as the team takes a break, he's on the pitch, slipping and sliding on the wooden surface, much to everyone's delight.

Ikon has also become a familiar sight in Aylesbury. Staff at Dixons, where John buys his printer cartridges, are used to Ikon standing up on his hind legs to pick up the right box in his mouth and hand it to John. How does he tell which one to get? John will say 'Get it!' and then, when he reaches the right one says 'That's it!' in that high-pitched tone he was taught to cultivate back in training class. John and Jennifer enjoy going to the cinema; so guess who goes too? Ikon usually dozes at the foot of John's wheelchair seat near the front of the screen; unfortunately, he's a loud snorer so John sometimes has to wake him up to keep him quiet. One of his favourite films was *Billy Elliott*, and his head always pops up if a dog appears on celluloid. Ikon was also a favourite at council committee meetings when John was on a board to promote facilities for the disabled. If the meeting went on for too long, Ikon would start 'chatting' – which made everyone look at their watches. If Ikon were a child, jokes John, he would have 'Talks too much!' written on his school report. At a recent demonstration with his brother Ivory in Bristol, Ikon had to be taken out because he kept interrupting the speaker, much to the crowd's delight. He also has one other vice – smelly feet.

So far, Ikon hasn't had to get John out of any real emergencies although he has been taught to respond to the spoken command 'Get help'. During the summer, John used this when he tried to pick up the barbecue lid and found it was slipping out of his grasp. Ikon ran in to get Jennifer; if he hadn't, the lid could have damaged John's legs. During their walks across the field, John sometimes gets stuck when it's muddy. At the word 'Push', Ikon will jump up and, using his front feet, push the chair forward. And when John had a flat tyre recently on the M40 as he was driving up to the Birmingham Bandits, it was comforting to have company as he waited on the hard shoulder for the AA to arrive.

Like most Canine Partners dogs, Ikon's first allegiance is to his partner. Although he tolerates Jennifer, and his ears will prick up when she comes home, Jennifer accepts that Ikon is a one-man dog. Sometimes, to wind him up, John will pretend to have a mock fight with Jennifer, and Ikon will come jumping in to interfere, barking madly. A few years ago, John might not have fooled around like this but Ikon has helped him relax. 'He's brought me out of myself and he's helped me to talk to other people. We're very different personalities but we also bring the best out in each other.'

It's the mark of a true friendship.

ELLA *and* JANET

One day, Nina Bondarenko received a phone call from a local breeder. This wasn't unusual; breeders often contact Canine Partners to see if they are interested in buying their puppies. But this one was different. She wanted to know why Canine Partners didn't take poodles. Nina explained it was because most poodle breeders don't like to release their dogs before three months, and Canine Partners liked to have their puppies as early as possible so they can commence with training. 'You can have one of my poodles at seven weeks,' said the breeder. Nina thanked her politely before pointing out that Canine Partners puppies also had to have the right temperament. 'Oh, mine has that, all right,' said the breeder enthusiastically. 'I'll come round and see you one day, shall I?'

Nina thought little more of the conversation until the

following week when the same breeder turned up unexpectedly at one of her puppy classes, holding a small black
poodle puppy. To Nina's surprise, she started joining in the
class, encouraging the puppy to do the exercises that the
other regulars were doing. 'What's she doing?' whispered
one of the trainers to Nina. 'She's not supposed to be here.
It's not an open class!'

But Nina could see that this small puppy was polite,
friendly and curious. She could see that this beautiful ebony
standard-poodle also had a delightful temperament. Then
Nina had a second surprise. 'Hang on to her for a moment,'
said the breeder. 'I've just got to get something from the car.'
She rushed back with a cheque for £250. 'I think your
charity is amazing,' she said. 'And I'd like you to have my
puppy as a gift – as well as this cheque.'

And that was how Ella came to be Canine Partner's first
poodle. It turned out that she was just as good at retrieving
objects as the retrievers and Labradors, which Canine
Partners usually selects. She also passed Nina's stringent
selection tests with flying colours, and this isn't easy. Canine
Partners' dogs really do have to be a cut above the rest. They
have to be highly intelligent and able to learn quite
complicated skills such as pressing a light switch with their
noses or paws. They need initiative to tackle tasks they might
not have been taught to do and yet their owner suddenly
needs them to do (such as helping to make the bed – something Ella later learned to do). They have to be constantly
aware of their partner's needs, always being on the alert.
And they also have to be highly reliable and stable – without
rushing off after rabbits or cats or anything else that takes
their fancy. All this takes a very special kind of dog with an
innate, natural talent – and Canine Partners feel that, despite
her unorthodox arrival, Ella might just have that 'IT' quality.
'She strutted her stuff,' says Alison Keeling, the after-care
officer. 'She was also very lady-like and stunningly good-
looking but also rather haughty, so we nicknamed her
Naomi Campbell.'

But when Ella went to live with her puppy-parent family, she began to show a more wilful side. It was as though, like a highly-paid super-model, she knew her worth and would only do something if it suited her. It was hard work for the puppy parent, but then something amazing happened. Ella struck up a bond with the family's youngest son who was partially deaf. Instead of skipping out of reach when asked to do something, Ella would do whatever this nine-year-old boy asked her to.

With anyone else, however, she was aloof to the point of being supercilious. 'If it was Tuesday and she worked on Tuesday, she would do it,' said Nina. 'But if it was Wednesday, she'd put her head to one side as though to say "I'm very sorry but I'm resting just now. I know I'm beautiful and to be honest, you're lucky that I'm honouring you with my presence."'

When Janet first met Ella she didn't feel particularly honoured. Forty-eight-year-old Janet Knowles has gone through more tragedy and disappointments in the last few years than most of us will, hopefully, ever know. As a young mother with two children aged five and six, her husband unexpectedly left her. For the next ten years, she struggled valiantly on her own and then fell in love again with some-one she met through her work for the blood transfusion service in Cambridge. They married in 1988, but in February 1994, Janet felt ill at work. She came home with a blinding headache and tried to eat dinner. Afterwards, her husband went upstairs to run a bath. When he came down, Janet was lying in a coma on the floor. She had had a stroke and a brain haemorrhage, caused by an aneurysm.

Janet was on a life-support machine for a fortnight and remained in a coma for a further two weeks. Her distraught children and husband were told to prepare themselves for the worst. Even if she recovered, she would be unlikely to walk or talk again. But they hadn't banked on Janet's deter-mination to pull herself back from the brink. Over the next year, through strength of character and intensive physiotherapy, she learned to walk again, in time to go to her daughter's wedding without having to use her wheelchair. But meanwhile, the operation to save her had cut through the optic nerve, leaving her with partial sight, so she could see only blurred outlines. She was also told that during the operation another aneurysm had been detected, although it was now being held in place with a wire coil, which would hopefully, prevent it from bursting.

Janet was left with a severe limp and lost the use of her left hand (she was a natural left-hander). She was forced to give up work and learn to cope with life as a registered blind person. One of the few things that helped was her dog, Ben, a one-year-old black Labrador, who provided companionship while her husband was out. Then, in 1996, her life fell to pieces again when her marriage to her husband broke down.

The next two years were the hardest of her life, even tougher than the months following her illness. Both her mother and sister, who live nearby, provided shoulders to cry on. But Janet was devastated. Nothing would ever be the same again. Then a friend suggested applying for a Guide Dog for the Blind dog. Janet, who still deeply missed her old dog, thought this was a wonderful idea. She spent nearly three days on a training course but was devastated to be turned down as, because of her disability, she found it difficult walking with a guide dog.

It would be enough to make many of us give up. But, Janet was determined to make the best of it. Then the same friend read an article about Canine Partners. Nothing ventured, nothing gained, thought Janet. Her social worker filled in the application form for her, as Janet is unable to write because of her illness. And to her excitement, Janet was invited on a one-day assessment course at Petersfield. 'It gave me a chance to walk a few dogs and use the commands, which we'd been given to learn. Ella was one of the dogs, but I wasn't very impressed by her. She seemed to take a long time to obey simple instructions like "Sit" or "Down". I thought "I hope I don't get this one because she's hard work." I also wasn't expecting a poodle.'

Instead, Janet had her eye on a golden retriever called Eddie who did exactly what he was told without having to be asked twice. When she was told that she would be accepted onto the forthcoming 12-day course where she might finally be teamed up with an assistance dog, Janet hoped she would get Eddie. But it was not to be. On the first day of the course, each dog was let into the room, one by one, and led to one of the hopeful recipients. To Janet's disappointment, Eddie's lead was given to someone else. Then a large black nose looked round the door as though searching for someone. It was Ella. 'There you are,' she seemed to say, spotting Janet lurking in the corner. And she made a beeline straight for her.

Janet's face, according to Nina, was a picture of horror. 'Why can't I have that one?' she asked, pointing to Eddie. 'Why do I get the poodle?' Meanwhile, Ella was all over her, as though to say 'I love you, I love you.' It was really quite funny, said Nina. 'She kept telling me that because Ella was black, she wouldn't be able to see her. So I told her I would get her a flashing collar. I really wanted Janet to give Ella a chance; a dog picks a person for a reason, and Ella was making it quite clear that she only wanted Janet. The trainers and I couldn't believe that Ella, who was always so aloof with everyone else, was falling over herself to do things for this woman who really wasn't interested in her.'

This 'picking' process is, in fact, another factor that makes these Canine Partners so special. We take it for granted that, as humans, we choose a dog. How else can it happen? But Canine Partners' dogs are so intelligent that for them it's the other way round. A partner might seem suitable on paper, but if the dog doesn't like that person, no way will the dog work with that partner. There's something almost mysterious about this, as Nina admits. 'There have been times when the dogs have really surprised me by picking people that I might not necessarily have thought they were suitable for. They do this by watching that person adoringly or sticking by his or her side, even if that person really prefers another dog. So when a dog shows that it likes someone, you have to take note. A dog is only going to do its best for a partner it loves and admires.'

This was definitely the case with Ella even though, as far as Janet was concerned, it was a case of unrequited love. Still, there was nothing for it. Janet was, after all, here to get a dog and if this was the one that Nina wanted her to try out, she had better get on with it. Reluctantly, Janet took Ella's lead and set about doing the exercises that would show whether they really were suitable for each other. She tried out general commands such as 'Let's go', which meant 'Let's go for a walk' and 'Better go now', meaning 'It's time to go to the lavatory'. Ella complied but, as in the previous session, she wasn't quick. Then the dogs were let off the lead in the paddock and their partners were instructed to call them back. Ella was the first dog to return, bounding straight up to Janet. Tears streamed down her face. 'She was impressed by Ella's devotion but she still couldn't bond with her,' explains Nina. 'I understood her reservations. After all, love isn't something that always comes instantly. But I advised her to give Ella the benefit of the doubt.'

Janet promised. But in the meantime, she was very moved by other people in her group. This is another lesson that Canine Partners recipients learn. For most of their lives, they have been suffering, often alone or, at best, with a loved one to help them. Now at the Canine Partners training centre, they are suddenly surrounded by others who have similar disabilities or restrictions but who share the same dream of making their lives more independent. Meeting such kindred spirits can be a great boost. One woman in Janet's group, who had been severely handicapped from the thalidomide drug, had trouble remembering the large number of commands. So every night, Janet sat in the bar with her, painstakingly going over each one. It helped her to remember them too. For example, to command a dog to get something off a shelf, you have to say 'Look, look'. You then focus your eyes on a tin or packet so that the dog focuses on the same object. Then you say 'Get it' and the dog will usually know what you mean and bring it to you.

During the first week, Janet felt she was getting a little closer to Ella but not as close as many of the other people in her group seemed to be with their dogs. 'This isn't working out,' she told herself. 'I'm going to have to try harder.' Maybe one way of doing it was to show Ella that she understood these exercises were a challenge for her, too. So when the group went shopping, as one of the exercises, Janet tried to choose items that Ella would find easy to get off the shelf. 'I came out with flannels and bath sponges that I didn't really want but which were simpler for Ella to "give" me in her mouth than hard tins.'

It worked. 'Well done,' Janet told Ella excitedly. Even better, the trainer praised them loudly, which made Janet feel good in herself. Even though these are grown men and women on the course, they are all tackling something new and it is rather like being back at school. Positive praise for the human partner as well as the dog, naturally goes a long way in building up self-esteem. Gradually, as the second week progressed, Janet could feel herself bonding more and more with the dog she had initially dismissed. As she went round Horsham on the shopping expedition that everyone has to do before graduating, Janet realised that Ella was giving her back the confidence she had lost after her illness. 'Before, when I went shopping, children would say "Why does that lady walk in a funny way?" But now people are looking at Ella first and me second.' For the first time in years, Janet was the centre of admiration and not of pity.

Ella also looked after her when Janet had to hold on to her while going down the stairs in the shopping centre. The other people in the course were in wheelchairs, so they had to do the lift exercise. But Janet was told to hold Ella firmly by the lead and take the stairs instead. It wasn't easy. Because of Janet's near-blindness, she had to rely on Ella totally to make sure that she didn't fall down. Ella, sensing the importance of her job, was extremely careful even when a child rushed by, brushing them to one side. To Janet's relief, she got down safely.

By now, Janet had decided that she really wanted to keep Ella. But would Canine Partners let her? She was delighted when told she had 'passed'. But after the graduation ceremony, Nina took her to one side. To Janet's distress, Nina explained that she could only have Ella on a month's trial. Someone from Canine Partners would visit her twice a week to see how she was getting on. Only then, if they were satisfied, would Ella be placed with Janet.

Once more, Janet was in floods of tears. What was the point, she wanted to know, of getting a dog if it might be taken away from her in a month? Janet wished she had never allowed herself to get attached to Ella. Now she was in danger of being hurt all over again. From Nina's point of view, however, it was the best decision. Nina still wasn't certain that Janet would be able to control Ella. 'We usually only get one failure in every six courses and that's because the person isn't physically able to cope with the dog or doesn't put the dog's interests first. Partly because of Janet's initial reluctance to accept Ella, I wanted to make sure they would work.'

At the time, Janet was living in a house with stairs but Ella adapted immediately. The Canine Partners worker who visited twice a week soon became a friend once she saw how devoted Janet and Ella were to each other and how easily Ella had made herself at home. By the end of the month, Janet was on tenterhooks. Then came the news she had so desperately wanted. Ella would be staying.

Janet was ecstatic and spent a small fortune on phone calls, ringing up her mother, sister and friends to give them the news. That was four years ago. Since then, Janet's quality of life has improved dramatically thanks to Ella, who now wears a yellow fluorescent collar with red flashing lights so Janet can see her more clearly. Going outside is no longer the terrible hurdle that it used to be, and Janet now has the confidence to get on a bus to Cambridge, some twenty miles away. The pair also walk to Sainsburys every Friday, which takes a good three-quarters of an hour. It's not easy with Janet's limp but she believes it's good exercise for both of them. Ella, acutely aware of her owner's limited sight, always moves out of the way of lampposts or obstacles in shops that might trip up Janet. Once, when Janet spotted her ex-husband who still lives nearby, she turned smartly round and walked off in the other direction. Ella, she says, helped her feel that she was no longer alone. Often, in the middle of the night, Janet – who is a poor sleeper – will take Ella for a walk around the Suffolk market town where she lives. The town is usually deserted at that time but Janet knows she is quite safe because Ella is a force to be reckoned with. Weighing 28 kilos, she is no pushover and acts as a substantial bodyguard for Janet during her nocturnal walks.

At home, Ella will tug at Janet's coat to help her off with it. This might seem a small task to those of us who do it without thinking. But for Janet, it's a great improvement on struggling out of her coat, unable to use one arm. Like many Canine Partners, Ella also uses her intuition. One day, watching Janet try to strip her bed, she began to tug at the corner of the sheets. Now, stripping the bed every Thursday is one of her regular jobs. It's an example of how a Canine Partner never stops learning. Who says you can't teach an old dog new tricks? These kinds of dogs are always open to something new. Rather like someone who's adept at crossword-puzzles, a Canine Partner thrives on a challenge. 'Well, well,' the dog seems to say thoughtfully. 'I need to pull a sheet across the mattress, do I? Odd thing to ask but I can do it without tearing the material if I hold it carefully in my mouth.'

Canine Partners dogs also learn through imitating.

Constantly alert, they see how things are done while living with someone. And if, one day, their human partner can't do something for some reason, they will try to do it instead. This has certainly been the case when Janet has passed out – something she has done three times, since getting Ella. On each occasion, Janet has come round to find Ella has brought her a mobile phone so she can call her mother. If she didn't have Ella as her personal alarm, she would feel very scared and vulnerable. 'Ella has seen me pick up the phone on enough occasions. So she simply did the same.'

Ella also loves Janet's mother, now in her early seventies, and her small Yorkshire terrier, Gemma, as well as her sister Lynda's dog, Penny. Last year, they all spent Christmas together. She adores, too, Janet's twin granddaughters, Bethany and Georgia, aged three. And when Janet couldn't find her mother in Homebase recently, she just said 'Find mother' and Ella led her to the right spot. 'You clever girl,' said Janet, bending down to give her dog a warm hug.

Ella goes everywhere with Janet, including her regular hospital check-up appointments. It was there that someone from a local golf club spotted her and thought she might be a worthy 'cause' for their fundraising activities. Unfortunately, by the time he tried to go up to her, she was called in for her appointment. But he left his name with the hospital, asking Janet to ring. She did, and was asked to talk to the club and appear at fundraising events. 'I was wined and dined and had a lovely time,' says Janet smiling. 'More importantly, we also raised £10,000 for Canine Partners.' This led to more fundraising activities for Newmarket Golf Club, which raised £5000 to train a dog. Friends working in a local factory have raised another £900, and her mother has collected £565 through line-dancing events.

Janet and Ella have recently moved to a beautifully converted flat in an old school building. As it's on one level, it makes it easier for both of them. 'Before, in the house I would throw my dirty washing down the stairs and Ella would carry each item into the washing machine for me.'

Despite being alone now that her children have left home, Janet is never lonely. As she sits on the sofa, watching television in the evening, Ella sits beside her with that beautifully straight back that any model would be proud of.

Ella never takes her eyes off Janet as she moves around her flat; and Janet can't bear to let Ella out of her sight. The only time that the pair are parted is twice a year when Ella has to have a general anaesthetic to have hair removed from her ear. This is crucial because, without the operation, she could become partially deaf and unable to hear Janet's commands. If she comes in from a walk, scratching her ear, Janet knows it's time to go to the vet. For Janet, it's agony being away from her, even for 48 hours, but she knows she has to go through this for Ella's health. It's a long way from the woman who hadn't wanted a 'mere' poodle.

Once a month, Janet is visited by Frank Hay, a local dog-trainer. In fact, Janet has known him since she was 15. Canine Partners always arranges a partnership linker for its placements; this is a dog expert who visits the recipients regularly to check everything is all right and act as an independent go-between for the partner and the charity. Janet suggested Frank, and now he has become a good friend.

'When I was 15, I never thought I'd be in this position,' says Janet, stroking Ella's beautifully clipped coat fondly. 'If I did, I would have been really upset. But now I can come to terms with it, because of Ella. We might not have hit it off at first but now she is everything to me. I'm not interested in getting married again. If you ask me, dogs are more reliable!'

BRIDIE *and* CAROLINE

Caroline Jarman was a pretty, vivacious young woman who was looking forward to a promising and rewarding career as a nurse at Whipps Cross Hospital in London, when a road accident changed her life for ever. One morning in 1988, as she was cycling to work, a van knocked her off her bicycle, sending her hurtling over the handlebars. Twenty-five-year old Caroline was plunged into a coma, and for the next three months no one knew if she would live or die. Her distraught parents sat by her bedside, talking constantly in the hope that their voices might 'wake her'. But when she did finally come round, Caroline discovered to her horror that she was paralysed down the right-hand side of her body. Although mentally alert she was, what is known as, a half-paraplegic. Not only was she confined to a wheelchair, she was also unable to talk clearly.

Suddenly, in the space of the few seconds during which

the van had sent her flying, Caroline's life and hopes for the future were shattered. For the next two years, she lived in the hospital rehabilitation unit, trying to come to terms with this terrible accident. One minute she had been a lively, popular girl who had loved going to parties and meeting friends. The next she was unable to walk and barely able to make herself understood.

Many young women whose lives had been changed like this would have been justifiably furious or depressed. But, although the accident had damaged Caroline's body, it had not taken away her determination. She went back to live with her parents in Essex for nearly five years but, during this time, decided to try to forge a more independent life. The local council helped by sending her to a special training centre for the disabled in Nottingham where she learned to do things like using her teeth to open margarine lids. It was very difficult for someone who had never before had trouble doing such simple tasks. But Caroline was simply not going to give up.

During her time at her parents, one of the things that helped keep her going was being with her parents' dog, Jasper. Her parents had had to employ a full-time carer called Jenny to help them with Caroline, and it was Jenny who recognised how much Jasper meant to Caroline. Somewhere, she seemed to recall, she had heard of a charity that trained dogs to help people like Caroline. She made several phone calls and finally tracked down Canine Partners and gave the details to Caroline and her parents.

In the meantime, Caroline was still trying to make herself as independent as possible. She knew she would have to have a full-time carer for the rest of her life, but like many young women in their early thirties, she desperately wanted a home of her own. At about this time, an adapted bungalow became available very close to her parents' home. It seemed an ideal solution. In fact, the move was more important than Caroline realised. When Canine Partners came to visit, they could see that Caroline had an ideal setting for an assistance dog. The bungalow had an adequate garden with enough space for a dog toilet, a necessity for Canine Partners' dogs who have their own fenced-in area. Caroline would also be able to take a dog for walks, provided the dog was totally reliable and wouldn't run off. And although Caroline had a full-time carer, an assistance dog would give her just that little bit more independence. Instead of waiting for her carer to come and pick something up off the floor or pass her the television remote control, she could ask a dog to do this for her.

Caroline was invited to join the Canine Partners training course but found it extremely tiring because of her severe physical injuries. The accident had also left her with short-term memory problems so it was hard to remember the ninety different commands, which she was meant to have memorised before the course. To make matters worse, one of the dogs that Caroline was being tried out with was not interested in her, and refused to respond to commands. So Nina substituted him with a beautiful golden retriever called Bridie. 'The dog had previously been partnered with a woman who had had multiple sclerosis so was used to being with someone whose movements were limited.'

As soon as Bridie's lead was given to Caroline, it was as though the final piece of the jigsaw had been put into place. Although Bridie had previously earned a reputation for being somewhat 'dizzy' and excitable, she seemed to turn over a new leaf when she saw Caroline. Caroline only had to give the word and Bridie would obey. She almost knew what to do before Caroline opened her mouth. Caroline could not believe it. Here was someone who understood what she was trying to say, despite her faltering speech. Not only that, but Bridie could do things for her that she had once been able to do herself but could no longer manage. It was, for her, nothing short of a miracle, and when the pair graduated at the end of the course, there wasn't a dry eye in the audience. The training had been a particular challenge for someone as severely disabled as Caroline – and everyone knew it.

It's impossible to exaggerate the importance of Bridie's arrival in Caroline's life. From a physical point of view, she could now help Caroline do some things she had once been able to do without thinking. Before the accident, Caroline had just moved down to London after completing her nursing training in Manchester. Quite naturally, she often rang her old friends and described her new life. Now, despite being unable to speak clearly, she still enjoys talking on the phone. And her friends and family have learned to understand her. But because she is unable to use her right hand at all and finds it difficult to hold things in her left, Caroline frequently drops the receiver. Before she had Bridie, she would have to wait until her carer could come and pick it up. But if the carer was out shopping, Caroline could only stare at the receiver lying on the floor in front of her, unable to explain to the friend at the other end of the line, what had happened. It was both frustrating and humiliating. Now, however, she doesn't even have to ask Bridie to get the phone. The dog instantly picks it up in her mouth and passes it to Caroline.

Before Bridie came, Caroline would also have trouble doing the simplest tasks such as putting on her own slippers. Now, when she drops them, because of her weak hand, there's no need to call out to Jenny or wait until she is free. Bridie simply picks them up for her and gently pushes them onto her feet. If someone is near and picks something up for Caroline before Bridie can get to it, she looks disappointed as though to say 'Hang on! That's my job.'

Bathtime, too, was a revelation. On their first day back, Caroline took a shower and was amazed when Bridie nosed her way into the bathroom. But when the dog picked up a corner of the towel in her mouth and brought it over to Caroline, she could hardly believe it. 'It was as though she could read my mind,' says Caroline.

Having Bridie there makes Caroline feel more independent and gives her that extra time alone that all of us need, whatever our abilities. Before Bridie moved in, Caroline had to lie in bed until Jenny or another carer was able to come and help her out. This was often frustrating and demeaning, especially if Caroline wanted to go to the bathroom. During her training, however, Bridie was taught to help Caroline get up by pulling the monkey pull from the foot of the bed up to Caroline so she can ease herself over the edge into her wheelchair.

Caroline also laughingly warns visitors to hang on to their purses. If they drop anything, Bridie will hand it to her! The only thing that she finds hard to pick up is the sweetner that Caroline takes in her coffee. When Caroline accidentally drops the tiny tablet packet on the floor, Bridie spends ages trying to find it because it's so small. 'Are you sure,' she seems to say, 'that there's really something down there?'

During those difficult years before Bridie, Caroline used to dread shopping. This, after all, was the town where she had grown up. Only a few years earlier, she had walked briskly down those pavements without thinking anything of it. But after the accident, when she had moved back with her parents, she knew all too well that people were staring at her in sympathy and curiosity. Now, however, with Bridie in her distinctive working coat, by her side, Caroline feels more confident in the knowledge that she is no longer alone. Together, the pair have become a familiar sight in local shops where Bridie is a dab hand at picking up tins and packets that Caroline cannot reach.

One thing that Caroline found particularly difficult was not being able to go out for walks in her chair unless someone was on hand in case she hurt herself. But now, with Bridie, Caroline can go out alone. Every day, she and Bridie go to the local park and play ball. Because Caroline is not strong enough to throw it herself, Bridie will take the ball up to a stranger and drop it at his or her feet. 'People look at me and seem to realise that I can't throw it,' says Caroline. 'So they do it for me. Then they start to talk to me, which is nice.'

Bridie and Caroline also enjoy sitting in the garden. As

happens to many wheelchair-users, Caroline's chair some-times becomes stuck in the grass. When this occurred before Bridie came into Caroline's life, she had to try to call out for her carer. This wasn't easy because Caroline's voice is weak and doesn't carry easily. Now, however, Bridie has learned to push and tug at Caroline's chair, rather like pulling a car out of the mud. Only a wheelchair-user can fully appreciate what a huge difference this has made.

Emotionally, Bridie is Caroline's best friend. Like all good chums, she's on the same emotional wavelength and seems to know when Caroline is feeling low. On bad days, when Caroline simply wants to lie down, Bridie will lie with her on the bed. 'I know how you feel,' she seems to say. 'But don't worry because I am here.'

Bridie also has an uncanny instinct for knowing which humans can be trusted and which can't. Recently, on the way back from the park one afternoon, Caroline heard a man walking behind them. 'Bridie went loopy and the man walked past quickly. I felt quite scared but also relieved because I knew she would look after me if anything happened. It's like having your own personal bodyguard.'

Even when Bridie is not performing a particular task for Caroline, she still prefers to stay by her side. One of Bridie's favourite resting positions is by Caroline's computer on which she types one-handed. Caroline loves reading but her short-term memory means that she often forgets the previous chapter. However, she has discovered by typing out what she has read, the story sinks in more. So every day, she painstakingly types while reading. Her current book is a novel by Ian Rankin, a choice that Bridie seems to approve of as she rarely disturbs her mistress.

It would be easy for someone like Caroline to stay at home all day. But Caroline is determined to make the most of what she can do. Before her accident, she enjoyed sports such as tennis and swimming. Now these are difficult for her but then she read about a trampolining club in Colchester that took disabled members. It was, for Caroline, a revelation, although it was not traditional trampolining as she used to know it. With this kind, she lay on the mat while helpers round the edge pressed the mat down to make it bounce.

When Bridie initially accompanied Caroline, she had to stay outside the hall with Jenny but she didn't like this. 'She was worried about me,' explained Caroline, 'because she didn't know where I was. Then they allowed her to come in and see me on the mat.When she realised I was all right, she settled down again. I also felt more relaxed, knowing she was there.'

Now that she is back in the area she grew up in, Caroline sees some of her old friends from the days before her accident. Her great friend, Catherine, often visits with her three children, all aged under ten. Bridie loves it when they come over, although Caroline jokes that they exhaust her so much that she sleeps for days afterwards. Bridie also enjoys a Sunday romp in the park when Caroline's father takes her, along with his own dog. But even though she enjoys the exercise, she still looks around as though to say 'Hang on, where's Caroline? Thanks for the game, boys, but I must be getting back.'

Most Canine Partners dogs seem to have at least one Achilles' heel or an area where they can't help slipping up. But Bridie really doesn't have one. She even got on perfectly well with Caroline's cat, partly, Caroline thinks, because Bridie's puppy-parent had a kitten. Both the cat and Bridie sleep on Caroline's bed, one on each side. 'Sometimes,' jokes Caroline, 'I worry that they will push me out of bed!'

If, before Bridie, someone had told Caroline how much a dog would change her life, she would have been sceptical. But now, her parents and her friends are amazed and thrilled at how much Bridie has helped Caroline. A good example is her new-found confidence to talk to total strangers in shops. 'The other day, a woman was staring at me. Before Bridie, I would have felt really embarrassed. But then I saw she was looking at Bridie's identification jacket, which explains she's a working dog, so I told her about Canine Partners. It made me feel good because she was genuinely interested in what I was saying and not just pretending to be polite.'

Just as important, Bridie has helped Caroline to come to terms with her disability. Many accident victims plunge into depression and some never recover. Caroline might have been one of those if it hadn't been for Bridie. After all, she knows all too well, that unlike her friend Catherine, she is now unlikely to marry or have children. It is a terrible fact for a young woman to have to accept. But somehow, Bridie has eased the pain. Having someone who is constantly beside her, and desperately keen to lavish affection on her and do what she wants, has made Caroline feel warm, wanted, and good in herself.

Caroline has also learned that, although there are many things she can no longer do, she has learned to master some new skills, such as teaching Bridie commands like 'Stay' and 'Draw the curtains'. This has given her a great sense of achievement and increased her self-esteem. Every day with Bridie brings something new. Last week, it was having the confidence to talk to a stranger in the post office, and next week, it will be something else. 'Bridie,' says Caroline, 'makes up for the parts of my body that don't work so well. There's really no one like her.'

GIBSON *and* ROY

It's 7 am and the radio alarm has gone off in the Capel household in Lee-on-the-Solent, Hampshire where 55-year-old Roy and his wife, Marian, lie in bed, gradually waking up. In the corner of their bedroom, there's a contented grunting noise as Gibson, a four-year-old retriever, turns over in his basket. But unlike his owners, he's faster at getting up. With a bound, he's at the bed, his chin pressed against Roy's side of the bed. 'Come on,' he seems to say. 'The sun is up. What are you waiting for?'

Roy has suffered from severe multiple sclerosis since his early thirties. At first, when his illness was diagnosed, he was able to walk on sticks, but as the years have passed, he is now a full-time wheelchair-user and is unable to stand. Even moving from his bed to his chair is a tremendous effort, which takes time and planning. Gibson knows all this but is prepared to wait. Once Marian has put his special sheet on the bed, he knows he can jump up and lie beside Roy: a special time whilst Marian gets dressed.

By 8.30, Roy is half-dressed and ready to hoist from bed to wheelchair. Together, Gibson and Marian help him get dressed. Roy's legs are very heavy for Marian to lift on her own, so after fetching Roy's shoes, Gibson uses his teeth to haul gently on Roy's trousers and lift them on to her knee so she can pull on her husband's socks and shoes.

Eight years ago, Roy could no longer use a stairlift, so with the help of Social Services and some very good friends a through-floor lift was installed. Before opening the door of the lift, on the command 'lift mode' Gibson settles down at the top of the stairs. Roy enters the lift in his wheelchair, and goes down to the lounge below. As the lift is too small for Gibson to be with Roy in the lift, he waits patiently until Roy is out of the lift and hurtles down the stairs as soon as he is called. At last, it's breakfast time. Gibson heads for his food bowl while Roy and Marian have cereal and toast. As he eats, Gibson raises his head every now and then to check that Roy is still there. Sometimes, he can't believe his luck that he's found someone like Roy. As a puppy, he had been rather over-anxious. He didn't like men carrying heavy objects although no one knew why. And he was, and still is, terrified by buzzing insects because he was stung by a bee at only three months old. Only now that he has a wonderful home of his own, does he feel really secure.

Marian and Roy met shortly before he fell ill. At the time, Roy was bringing up his seven-year-old son Dominic after the break-up of his first marriage, and Marian had recently returned from Australia to recover from her broken marriage. They fell in love immediately and married the following year. Then, in 1982, two months before their son Tim was born, Roy was diagnosed as having multiple sclerosis. It was a cruel blow for a couple who had only just found happiness. But Marian and Roy decided they would try to be positive. 'We're still madly in love,' says Marian. 'When you care for someone, you just have to get on with any difficulties that come up.'

Meanwhile, the couple try to live as normal a life as possible under such circumstances. Marian runs her own business, selling books in schools. She usually leaves home around lunch-time, so whilst she is answering the telephone and packing boxes of books into the van, Roy attaches Gibson's lead to his chair and sets out for the local recreation ground which is only a short walk away. This is another of Gibson's favourite times and he walks along happily wagging his tail. He's always enjoyed walks since he was a puppy when he was looked after by Mandy Lebbon, his puppy-parent and a mother of three from Chichester. She used to carry him in a rucksack, against her chest so she could walk her other dog at the same time. The warmth of her body made him feel secure.

Meanwhile, down at the recreation ground, Gibson will be enjoying his playtime with his doggy friends. Roy will throw a ball for Gibson who loves bringing it back to him. Passers-by often stop to look at the fun the two are having. The bond between man and dog shines out like a beacon, but what strangers don't know is that when Roy and Gibson first met at a Canine Partners training session, it didn't look as though they were going to make it as a team. Roy had heard about Canine Partners through a local speaker at his local multiple sclerosis centre. Having already had one dog, who had since died, he was keen on having another who could also help him round the house.

But soon after making his application, Roy's MS became worse. By the time he got to the training centre to see if he was a suitable candidate, his hands had become increasingly weak and floppy. Nina tried him out with Gibson, but Roy found even the simplest tasks hard to handle. His weak hands even made it difficult for him to take Gibson's lead on and off, as instructed. The weather was also very hot, which exacerbated Roy's symptoms. By lunch-time, he was so tired that he had to give up and go home. Not only was it utterly frustrating for a man who used to be a five-handicap golfer, it was also a bitter blow. Although he had only met Gibson briefly, this beautiful golden retriever had made a huge impression on him. If only he had been strong enough to cope.

Canine Partners gave Roy another chance, a few months later, on a two-day course. Gibson wasn't there then but, nevertheless, Roy was desperate to have one of these wonderful dogs who could help him so much by turning on lights, picking up the pens he was constantly dropping, opening doors and bounding up stairs to get keys. But again, Roy simply wasn't physically able to complete the course. Utterly dejected, he returned home.

During the following two months, he kept thinking about Gibson. It was as though something was telling him not to give up, however badly the odds were stacked against him. Marian decided to write to Canine Partners suggesting that, as they lived so close, Roy could train during the morning only. But Nina had a better idea. It was unusual but, given the circumstances, the charity could go to Roy's home and train him on the spot. Alison Keeling, the after-care officer, spent two weeks helping Roy and Gibson work together. Because Roy couldn't hold out the collar to Gibson, she brought a specially-made loop collar and lead, which Gibson learned to put his own head through. Not all dogs could learn to do this but it's an example of how these Canine Partners dogs will tackle any new challenge. Alison also went through the usual training paces and took them down to the local shops where Gibson learned to touch-paw food items down from the shelves, 'hand over' the wallet at the till and sit quietly at the pelican crossing.

During the following two months, after they had passed the final qualifying test, Alison continued to visit regularly to help Gibson learn extra tasks. To teach him to open a door leading to Roy's computer room, for instance, she attached some sticky tape to the door frame. Using the word 'Nudge' as a command, she said the word clearly and then looked hard at the tape. Following her eyes, Gibson touched the tape with his nose. As he did so, Alison used a clicking machine to make a noise and gave him an edible treat at the same time. In this way, Gibson associated the command 'Nudge' with the clicking noise and the treat. If he wanted that tasty chew, all he had to do was push open the door.

Now, as the pair make their way home from their walk to the house, both Roy and Gibson cannot imagine life without each other. It's almost 11 am and time for Roy to do a bit of paperwork. Marian's small business is essential for the family budget, and although Roy's restrictions mean he can only help in a limited way, he is able to do some of the accounts. Roy also enjoys writing at this time of day. Recently, he published his own guide to coping with disability* and he also writes poetry.

Gibson, too, takes a great interest. As Roy writes, he sits next to him, watching every move or, if he's feeling tired, having a nap. Gibson has also learned to take paper from the computer feeder and hands it to Roy. Like other Canine Partners dogs, he is constantly on the alert for anything that goes beyond the call of duty. During his second week at the Capel house, Gibson was sitting in the garden, happily chewing his bone. Through the French windows, he suddenly saw that Roy had dropped his mobile phone by the desk. He came immediately with the bone in his mouth. Without hesitation, he put his forepaws onto Roy's lap and gently gave him the bone. He then dropped back down, picked up the telephone and gave it to Roy in his other hand. Roy passed him back the bone, and Gibson trotted off back to the garden. 'It was incredible,' said Roy.

By now it's almost one o'clock and time for lunch. Maggie, who comes to help in the house while Marian is out, makes Roy a ham or cheese sandwich. Gibson sits by his side but, unlike most dogs, doesn't ask for a titbit. Adorable as these dogs are, it's vital that they don't overstep

---

How to Reduce Your Handicap: A Guide to Coping with Disability by Roy Capel. Pennyquick Publishing

the boundaries. They are, after all, working dogs as their red coat shows.

After lunch, Roy has a long nap in his reclining electric wheelchair in the sitting room. Gibson sits quietly at his feet, snoozing. But when Roy wakes up, at about 4 pm, Gibson is at the ready. He jumps up on his hind legs and carefully removes the pillows from behind Roy's back. Again, this isn't something he was taught by Alison; it's a skill which he learned himself from watching Maggie or Marian doing it.

Roy takes great pride in the incredible things that Gibson can do. Often, after his afternoon nap, he'll practise certain tasks with his dog, such as opening and shutting doors. 'Even though he's been doing this ever since he got here, I still get a real thrill out of seeing him do things that ordinary dogs couldn't do.'

When Marian returns at about 5.30 it's time for another walk. It's an ideal opportunity for Marian to tell Roy about her day as Gibson walks by the side of the chair, one ear cocked, always listening. The Capels live in good dog-walking country, five minutes from the seafront, which has a wide concrete walkway, adjacent to the beach and ideal for a wheelchair and dog. Recently, however, Roy had a shock when during a walk without Marian, his chair got stuck in a gully down a side road. He had just gone past a pub but was too far to call out for help. Canine Partners dogs are trained to bark on command but Gibson had rarely been asked to do this. Would he remember?

'Bark!' instructed Roy. 'More, more.' To his relief, Gibson started barking, and within five minutes an elderly lady heard the noise through her upstairs window and came down to see what the fuss was about. She went into the pub and emerged with two tough men who freed Roy's chair. There was only one problem: the wheel was broken. So they phoned Marian and, while waiting for the van to arrive, bought Roy a drink from the pub. 'If Gibson hadn't been able to bark like that, I could have been stuck for a long time,' says Roy.

By seven o'clock it's generally suppertime. On Saturday nights, Roy and Marian enjoy an Indian take-away while Gibson enjoys his weekend bone. They'll then watch television with Gibson at their feet or listen to music. Recently, Roy has taken up the mouth organ, one of the few instruments he can hold, and Gibson is fascinated by the high-pitched notes. 'He stands on his hindlegs and tries to sit on my lap so he can get closer.'

Sometimes, Roy likes to move from his chair to the sofa. This is a complicated process. First he has to be strapped into a harness and then be hoisted along runners, built into the ceiling, before he can be lowered. Again, Gibson will help attach the harness by taking it into his mouth.

During non-working days, Roy and Marian might drive up to Warwick University to visit their son Tim or down to Wales where Dominic lives with his wife and children. Five years ago, the Capels' friends and family raised several thousand pounds to buy a van that was large enough to take Roy's chair. It has made a huge difference to their lives and Gibson loves riding in the back.

Come 10.30 pm and it's time to get ready for bed. Roy wheels his chair into the lift-corner of the sitting room, and within minutes he's back in his bedroom. Meanwhile, Gibson has run upstairs to join him. It's a reversal of what has happened in the morning and sometimes it's hard to believe that a whole day has gone by so fast.

Roy often lies awake for a while, listening to Gibson gently snoring in his basket. It's at quiet times like this that Roy's poems often come into his head. One called 'My Dog', shows how much joy, hope and meaning Gibson has brought to Roy's life:

Gibson, my dog, helps with many a task.
He leaps into action whenever I ask.
He brings me the paper and all of the mail,
Fetches my shoes, with a wag of his tail.
He brings his bowl when it's time to feed.

127

When we go out, he fetches his lead.
Shopping now is less of a chore
Gibson comes with me to the village store.
If there are goods I can't reach myself
Then Gibson will pick them off the shelf.
He takes my purse up to the till
Puts paws on the counter and pays the bill.
At pelican crossings, when at the shops
He presses the button so the traffic all stops.
He loves a good run when we go to the park
When we get home, I tell him to bark.
Someone opens the door and when I say
He takes off my hat and puts it away.
Helping like this is something he loves.
He tugs off my coat, my scarf and gloves.
He picks things up that I drop on the floor
Turns on the light and opens the door.
At times of stress or apprehension,
Stroking Gibson can ease my tension.
On mutual respect we can both depend.
He's my dog, my partner, a faithful friend.

BERTIE *and* NATALIE

Dirtie Bertie is a smart golden retriever with a passion for dirty puddles – hence his nickname. So smart, in fact, that he is one of the few Canine Partners dogs to have gone to university. Not long ago, he was a familiar sight at Essex University where, along with many other students, he would fall asleep during lectures and wake up with sudden loud yawns that set everyone laughing. Bertie was also a regular at the union bar along with his partner, Natalie Meadows, a young woman in her thirties, who was reading politics. And when Natalie graduated in 1998, Bertie walked along the platform with her to receive her degree certificate.

None of this surprised Nina Bondarenko who knew as soon as she spotted Bertie at a breeder's kennels in Dorchester that this was one very clever dog. Interestingly, he was the only puppy in the litter who was suitable; when Nina tested the others, some just sat still. Bertie, on the other hand, was keen to do everything he was asked. However, as is often the case with intelligent animals, there was one big catch. Bertie knew he was clever. He was used to adulation. and he was extremely self-interested, which might mean he would be unsuitable when it came to putting someone else first. 'Bertie was the kind of dog,' recalls Nina, 'who would amuse himself at the trainer's expense. He would stand and smile until a door opened, and then he would disappear, preferably into woods or whatever other land was nearby.' The trainers would think he had escaped but Nina could see him peeping through the bushes like a naughty child. 'He was attention seeking. Simple as that. He wanted us to come and find him.' If Nina could get Bertie over that preoccupation with himself, he could make an extremely clever assistance dog. If not, it would be a great waste of Canine Partners' time and resources. It was a risk she was prepared to take but she desperately hoped that it would pay off.

The first glimmer of hope came during the intensive training programme that all puppies go through before being teamed up with a partner. Nina had taught Bertie to take articles from her hand and place them in a wheelchair basket. One day, a bigger and more old-fashioned wheelchair arrived for them to use in this exercise. At first Nina didn't realise the basket was too high for Bertie to see. When she instructed him to put her purse in the basket, Bertie gave her a puzzled look before trotting round the back and front of the chair, searching. First he put the purse in the gap between the axle and the back of the chair. No, that wasn't right. What about the battery compartment? By this time, he'd attracted an audience of trainers, fascinated by this dog who refused to give up. Suddenly, Bertie looked up and saw what he had been looking for. Leaping up, he dropped the purse into the elusive basket, and ran around the chair several times as though performing a lap of honour. 'I did it,' he seemed to be saying. 'Not easy but I got there!'

In 1996, Bertie was then homed with Freddie, a frail lady in her late sixties. They worked well together, but a few months after Bertie arrived, Freddie had a bad fall. 'Bertie instinctively brought her blanket to keep her warm and her mobile phone,' describes Alison Keeling, Canine Partners' after-care manager. 'If it hadn't been for Bertie, Freddie would not have got help so fast.' Sadly, Freddie was too ill to continue having Bertie so he was brought back into the Canine Partners centre for a refresher session and put on the next training course.

Unknown to Bertie, however, he was about to meet some-one else who was also as bright he was. Natalie Meadows was born with spinal muscular atrophy and had been in a wheelchair from the age of 11. In spite of her physical disability, Natalie has always remained outgoing and lively. After school, Natalie, who lived in Chichester with her mother, worked at a local hospital as a clerical officer. It was pretty routine work but there was one light in Natalie's life – a little Yorkshire terrier called Disney owned by Natalie's mother. When Disney died at age ten, Natalie kept thinking it would be nice to get another dog. By coincidence, she happened to see a programme on television about a dog-training scheme in Holland to help people like her. Even more coincidentally, her occupational therapist knew of a charity currently being set up in the UK to do something similar. The charity called Canine Partners, was looking for dogs to train and people to team them up with. Would Natalie be interested?

She was tempted, but realised it was totally impractical. Natalie had already decided she needed more out of life than a clerical job. She wanted to read politics at university and was hoping to get a place at Essex. It would be impossible to have a dog there, especially as she would be living in a hall of residence with other students, without a garden or the other features that a Canine Partner would need. Natalie did, however, agree to be photographed with some of the Canine Partners dogs in training, to help the charity with its pro-motional work. 'I thought the dogs were lovely,' she said, smiling as she always does. 'And I couldn't help thinking that maybe, I'd be in a better position one day to have one.'

At the age of 25, Natalie then went off to Essex but she never forgot those dogs who had sat so obediently by her chair while the Canine Partners photographer took his shots. Still, she'd made the right decision, she kept telling herself. Natalie's sharp brain thrived on the challenge of university life even though her ill-health meant that she constantly had to take time off during the course. By the time she had reached the end of her second year, some six years later than normally expected, Natalie knew she had to give her body a break. She asked permission to take a full year out before going back to complete that final year. During that time, she applied for – and got – a council house near the university and it just happened to have a garden suitable for a dog. It was finally time to contact Canine Partners.

Because Nina already knew Natalie, she didn't have to go on all of the day-long assessment courses. Instead, she went straight on to the 12-day course at Brinsbury College in Sussex. That evening, Natalie was looking out of her bedroom window when she saw two chocolate Labradors and a golden retriever on leads in a van. 'The Labradors were leaping all over the place like mad muppets,' said Natalie. 'But the golden retriever was just sitting there, looking around him calmly, with his tail wagging. I couldn't help thinking that I would really love that one.'

The following day, she and the other recipients on the course were taken into a large room and the dogs were then let in. To her joy, Natalie's wish was granted and she was given Bertie, the beautiful golden retriever she had glimpsed the night before. Natalie tried to remember all the commands she'd been taught and was pleased that Bertie seemed to obey her. What she couldn't understand was how everyone else around her seemed amazed that Bertie was doing what he was told. She didn't know that Bertie had a reputation for being stubborn. As Natalie continued her exercises with Bertie, he seemed to flourish. She only had to say 'Up' and he would reach whatever she was asking him to get. Nina and the other trainers could hardly believe it. They say that the dog picks the person and this was proof. Bertie had fallen head over heels for Natalie – and she for him. Both felt right for each other and everyone agreed they were a natural match.

Natalie could hardly believe her luck. She felt safe with this dog. She could even take him on walks round the grounds, knowing that he would never take off with her. She also managed to do the mock test around town in which Bertie had to stay down for three minutes while Natalie wheeled herself out of sight. Sceptics might say that Bertie's love was fuelled by the treats Natalie saved for him from breakfast but Natalie knew it was more than that. 'It's true that I hid bits of bacon from the huge fry-ups we had every morning,' she said with a twinkle in her eye. 'You're not meant to give them titbits but I couldn't help it. I wanted to tell Bertie he was behaving brilliantly.'

At night, Bertie would sneak onto Natalie's bed even though he was meant to lie down in his own at the foot of hers. One evening, Natalie was lying in the bath when he came pottering in and drank some of the bubbles. 'When I told the staff, they couldn't believe it. Apparently Bertie absolutely hates bathrooms and will normally never go in them. But he didn't seem to mind this time because he wanted to reach me and have a chat.'

At the time, Natalie had two care assistants called Tasha and Julia who lived with her, taking it in turns to be on duty. They, too, came on the course to help care for Natalie although they were in different rooms. As part of the Canine Partners training, Nina understandably wanted to make sure that Natalie would cope if it was just her and Bertie together. And she did. 'It was such a lovely feeling not to have anyone else but him,' said Natalie. Like all of us, she needs her privacy, for the first time in her life she was able to have that thanks to Bertie. Until he had arrived, Natalie had constantly needed someone at hand, in case she needed something, and this could often be restricting. But here was someone who could allow her space and also care for her, keep her company and be her friend. It was a unique relationship.

One of the incredible things about Canine Partners dogs is that they can be taught extra tasks to adapt to their partners' individual special needs. Natalie's hands are twisted and limp so she doesn't feed herself well and finds it difficult to pick things up. Bertie isn't able to help with feeding but the basic Canine Partners training has already taught him to pick up, in his mouth, anything that Natalie drops ranging from a piece of paper to a book. But unlike the other people on the course, Natalie even found it hard to slip the collar round Bertie's neck, so Nina taught him, in five minutes, to put his own head through the lead and then take it off again. She also taught him to move Natalie to a more upright sitting position and to take off her hat, scarf and gloves – something he continues to do to unsuspecting visitors. He learned, too, to position his feet carefully on Natalie's metal footplate without resting on her feet, before jumping up to give her something. 'When he first tried to give her her gloves, she yelped with pain,' recalls Nina. 'Then we realised that he was standing on her feet; because Natalie bruises easily, her feet were black and blue. So we had to teach him to stand on a tiny bit of the frame that was empty. To our amazement, he did it.' Such an achievement was not just down to Bertie for being so quick on the uptake. It was also thanks to Nina who has a special talent for seeing what is needed at a glance and then training the dog to do it.

Then, just as it all seemed to be going well, disaster struck. Natalie developed her familiar sciatica pains and chest infections. Despite a heavy course of antibiotics, she had to go to bed for two days during the second week of the course. Natalie was in floods of tears because she thought she wouldn't be able to complete the course. She really loved Bertie and was certain from the way he followed her around that he loved her too. Now because she was ill, they were finished. Then Nina came to see her. 'I've been watching you both together and I've decided you should both go home,' she said gently. Natalie could hardly believe it. It was extremely rare for anyone to be allowed to graduate early without actually finishing the course. But Nina felt that Natalie and Bertie had earned their colours. Besides, it was nearly time for the new university year to start and Bertie was ready to join Natalie as a mature student.

Thanks to the university's policy of equal opportunities, the Dean of Students at Essex gave his permission for Bertie to attend lectures and seminars with Natalie. However, some of the tutors looked a little doubtful at first. How did they know that a dog was not going to disturb serious seminars in which students would be discussing weighty political arguments? They need not have worried. Bertie usually went to sleep at Natalie's feet, waking only when she needed to go to another lecture or seminar and have help in opening those heavy university doors. Besides, politics really wasn't Bertie's scene as he made clear when he yawned loudly halfway through the lecture when he was getting a little too warm and comfortable.

'The other students thought he was wonderful,' said Natalie laughing. 'Lots of people came up to me who wouldn't have done otherwise to stroke him, even though you're not really meant to do that to assistance dogs because they're working. Many of my friends said he reminded them of the dogs they'd left behind at home; it helped them to get over their homesickness by cuddling Bertie. Canine Partners like Bertie truly are an amazing way of meeting new people and breaking down barriers. It's surprising how many friendships have developed because people own a dog. After all, it's easy to walk past someone you don't know but much harder to walk past a four-legged stranger who is staring up at you adoringly and begging you to scratch his ears!'

At Natalie's graduation ceremony, attended by her mother and sister, staff offered to escort her over the platform in case Bertie didn't like the clapping. Natalie assured them that Bertie would actually love the praise and assume it was directed entirely at him. True to form, Bertie took the ceremony in his stride. 'Thank you,' he seemed to say. 'Yes, I have worked exceptionally hard for this degree.'

Natalie then got a job working with a disability equality trainer before going on to work for the Essex Coalition for Disabled People. This involves making several home visits a week and giving advice on how to use the government grant to 'buy' services such as full-time carers. Bertie goes with Natalie and her carer; not only does he help her practically by opening doors, he also helps break the ice. 'He's used to wheelchairs so he can go right up to people and let them stroke him,' points out Natalie. 'Many of them haven't been able to do this before and their faces really light up.' Bertie's presence has also spread the word about Canine Partners. So far, at least three of Natalie's acquaintances have asked for more information on the scheme.

Alison Keeling describes Bertie as an opportunist who will seize the moment if he thinks something can be gained. 'If Natalie occasionally forgets to get his meal, he'll go and get his bowl for her.' Occasionally, Bertie's stubborn streak will surface; he can, for instance, be rather naughty with Natalie's care assistants, pretending not to hear them when they call or refusing to respond to a 'Down' command. He also has a wicked sense of humour and will frequently wake Natalie by picking yesterday's underwear off the floor and pushing it in her face. Bertie also enjoys a good party and loves it when Natalie takes him out. Several of her university friends still live near by and he particularly loves watching them dance. Fooling around on the floor in mock fights is, however, a different matter. 'What on earth are you doing?' he'll seem to say as he tries to pull them apart. He is, however, more than understanding when Natalie's friend's nephew, Ben, age three, tries to ride him. 'It's not in my job description,' he sighs, 'but I'll do it, just for you.'

Sometimes Natalie jokes that her friends come to see Bertie rather than her. There's certainly always a queue of people arriving to visit. When one of her friends, Sarah, took Bertie for a walk, Natalie received a panic call because he had begun to limp, inexplicably, on the way back to the car. Sarah took Bertie to the vet where he put his own paws up on the bed to be X-rayed. Then came the bombshell. 'They told me there was a possibility that he might have cancer and that we would not know for a week,' said Natalie. It was the longest week of her life but by the following week, when Natalie and Sarah took him for his next X-ray, he was already walking without a limp. Bertie had merely strained something; it was a false alarm but it was not something that Natalie wanted to go through again.

When Natalie isn't working, she and Bertie frequently do demonstrations together to help raise public awareness about the charity. Natalie really enjoys this; never one to sit still for long, she enjoys having a job to do. 'It also gives me the chance to put something back into an organisation that has helped me so much.' Bertie, too, loves performing, although Natalie often has to warn the audience to watch out for their gloves. If there's a spare one lying around, Bertie will get it.

After work is over, the best part of the day is snuggling up together in front of the television. 'Sometimes I can't believe how lucky I am to have Bertie,' says Natalie, as she kisses the end of Bertie's nose. 'The last four and a half years have been the happiest of my life. It's amazing what a difference a dog can make.'

HAZEL *and* SARAH

Sarah Ashcroft is a pretty young woman in her early twenties. Like many girls of her age, she loves discos, shopping with friends and adventurous holidays ranging from abseiling to yachting. There is, however, one big difference that makes Sarah stand out from her friends. Sarah has been a wheelchair-user since the age of two when she was diagnosed as having mild cerebral palsy, caused by her premature birth. As a result, she is unable to stand unsupported, although she can speak clearly and is bright and intelligent.

Sarah is an example of how far Canine Partners has come since its conception in the early 1990s. When the charity was first founded, it was assumed that it would help people who were severely disabled and totally dependent on their care assistants. As it evolved, however, it became clear that it could also help people who were reasonably independent but who still needed that extra help. It has also begun to draw in younger applicants like Sarah who, in turn, can pass on the word about Canine Partners to friends in the same age group. This helps to publicise the charity among the wider circles, especially big firms such as Abbey National, British Gas, Tesco and John Lewis who, amongst others, have recently helped to sponsor Canine Partners dogs.

Another benefit, which has come to light, is the peace of mind that a Canine Partner can give to the care assistant or family member. The dog frees the carer from many routine tasks such as picking up things or opening doors or turning on lights and it also provides great reassurance because the carer knows the dog can get a phone or press an emergency button in any emergency. 'Since the dogs are virtually on "stand-by" most of the time, the care assistant or carers involved can relax because they are no longer on-call 24 hours a day,' points out Nina Bondarenko. 'The quality of that person's life improves significantly.'

Sarah lives with her mother in Kent but has always been encouraged to do as much as she could. 'She started going abroad on holiday with friends when she was a teenager,' says her mother. 'She also works in an office and loves going out to parties. Most of her friends are able-bodied and we've tried to live as normal a life as possible. But she'd always hankered after a dog, partly because my parents had a border collie whom she loved to play with. To be honest, I thought it was impossible because we lived in an upstairs apartment without a garden. I also felt we had enough on our plates without this extra commitment.'

At the time, Sarah was doing voluntary work for the charity Dial. One day, she spotted an advertisement on the noticeboard for a demonstration of Canine Partners dogs. Although Sarah had never heard of Canine Partners, she went along. Sarah will never forget what she saw. 'The demo was done by a Labrador called Eddie and his owner, Denise. Like everyone else who was watching, I thought it was really sweet when the dog picked up keys and a mobile phone when Denise told him to.'

Sarah also knew that she was more able than most

disabled people to do these things for herself. 'But I really liked the idea of having a dog around. If I hadn't been a wheelchair-user, we would probably have had one of our own anyway. Now I had seen what these dogs could do, I felt there was no reason why we shouldn't have one too.'

In order to be eligible for a Canine Partner, however, the Ashcrofts had to move to a house with a garden so, within a few weeks, they found a suitable adapted house near Ashford in Kent. Sarah promptly filled out Canine Partners forms, while at the same time preparing herself for a long wait. She had known, through talking to the organisation, that it could take months and even years before she was teamed up with a dog. She was also aware that this might not even happen if she wasn't considered suitable during the training course.

Three months later, Sarah was called to the Petersfield training centre for an introductory assessment day. Hazel was one of the first dogs she was teamed with and Sarah thought she was very pretty. In fact, although Sarah didn't know this, several people commented on how similar the two were with their blonde colouring and slight builds. Sarah noticed that when Hazel worked with the men on the course, she didn't always obey promptly. 'It was as if she preferred to be told what to do by a woman. I could see that Hazel was very sensitive to someone's tone of voice. She didn't like being bullied or shouted at. But at the same time, you had to be firm in a quiet way.'

Sarah's observations were extremely acute. Hazel had, in fact, already earned the nickname Fizz-Brain because of her behaviour. One minute she was dizzy, loopy and excitable. And the next, she was on perfect behaviour, happily turning on light switches or pawing down a tin from a supermarket shelf.

Since the charity's conception, Nina has had the gift of teaming the right dogs with the right person. Over the years, she has also learned to fine-tune this natural gift. Hazel could be perfect for the right person who was able to control this dizziness. But she would be disastrous for someone who couldn't. In some ways, this makes Canine Partners dogs more realistic. In the early years, the dogs were often seen as paragons who would do all these amazing chores without faltering. Now, however, it is recognised that dogs are like humans. There are times when they don't actually want to do something; and part of the challenge is to find ways to encourage them to comply.

As a puppy, Hazel had had a puppy parent who had done just this. Sue Wilkinson already had her hands full with her daughters aged seven and only 18 months. But, like many puppy-parents, she wanted to help this unusual charity by offering a dog a temporary home and helping to train it. 'We loved Hazel even though she sometimes drove us mad with her exuberance. She was also very funny. At the time we had three cats, and Hazel decided that perhaps she was really a cat after all. She'd drape herself over the back of a chair as our cats did and then stretch out. She loved swimming in my sister's pool and would jump onto air mattresses and frighten everyone. She also enjoyed sitting on our garden trampoline and waiting for someone to bounce it. When she was good, she was very, very good. But when she didn't want to do something, it was hard trying to persuade her.'

Hazel's erratic behaviour meant she did an extra three months in advanced training after her time with the Wilkinsons. She was also tried out with several people at the centre (and stayed with Ian Free who later had Ivory), but no one seemed to be able to get her to truly focus. Then along came Sarah.

During that initial day, Sarah did simple assessment exercises with two other dogs as well as Hazel. 'I liked her but we had been told, so many times, that we shouldn't allow ourselves to get attached until we knew who we were getting, that I had to force myself to be objective.'

To her delight, Sarah was invited to go back to the training centre for further assessment sessions and Hazel was there. 'I liked her more and more as the day went on. I could see that she was quiet and that she didn't jump up like some of the others. She also had a really pretty face that seemed to say "I like you too."'

After that, came yet another one-day session. This is something else that the charity has learned. Sometimes it's possible to see a potential match between a dog and partner after only one training day. But on other occasions, like this, Nina needs to see them more often to be certain. She was right to be careful. That day Hazel was not her usual perfect self for Sarah. First, she didn't always come back to Sarah during the re-call exercises. And later, she refused to go through a door as instructed. 'You're taught to use a high-pitched voice to make the commands and I tried to do that,' recalls Sarah. 'But Hazel didn't want to listen. In the end, one of the trainers got her to do it but it dented my confidence. I felt miserable all the way home. I had managed all my life without a dog, but since seeing Hazel, I felt my life could be improved. Now I was frightened I was going to lose her.'

Nina was concerned, too. 'Sarah was very timid. When she first arrived, we could barely get a word out of her. I kept wishing she could be a bit more assertive, and when I could see what was happening with Hazel, I told her that there was no point in carrying on if she wasn't firmer. Sarah burst into tears, but sometimes you have to be tough to be kind.'

Sarah still wasn't sure and was upset all the way home. She knew that if she couldn't get her confidence back, it would deeply affect her ability to instruct Hazel next time she saw her; if, indeed, there was a next time. Canine Partners recipients have to be firm and confident, otherwise a dog can pick up their insecurities and fail to respond properly.

It might have been the end of all Sarah's dreams if the training staff had not decided to try some different forms of assessment. Alison, one of the trainers, rang the Ashcrofts and asked if she could bring Hazel down for the day to visit them. It was the best thing she could have done. Hazel walked into the Ashcrofts' new home and immediately headed for the garden, where she bounded round in excited circles before coming back and sitting by Sarah's feet. 'I'm back,' she seemed to say. 'Now what would you like me to do next?'

It was the confidence booster Sarah needed. When she was called back to the training centre the following month for a 12-day residential course, Sarah was determined to rise to the challenge. 'I'm going to do this,' she told herself. 'We're going to make it as a team.'

One of the highlights of the course, for Sarah, was taking Hazel for walks outside. 'Although I was used to going out in my chair on my own, it was wonderful to have a dog who kept looking back up at me to check I was all right. I also felt good when people began to look at me. Before Hazel, they would stare because they were curious and knew that they didn't want to be like me. Now they were staring because I had something they actually wanted and admired – Hazel. It made me feel special in a way that I had never felt before.'

Hazel began to obey Sarah in a way that she rarely obeyed anyone else. Sarah isn't quite sure why, but she remembered what Nina had said about the dog choosing the person and not the other way round. Perhaps, Sarah thinks, Hazel identified with her. Both are blonde and alike in their stubborn but quiet personalities. They were both born under the star of Taurus the bull (characteristics include determination) and have May birthdays.

To her relief, Sarah and Hazel passed the final test at the end of the course. But she was apprehensive about how Hazel would behave when she took her home. On the course there was always someone on hand to ask for advice. But now this was for real. Unlike some of the other partnerships, there wasn't anyone else nearby with a Canine Partner with whom Sarah could swap notes. However, she did know that one of the trainers would be in weekly contact for the first month and then every three months. She also knew she could pick up the phone for help, any time.

But Sarah's worries were unfounded. As soon as Hazel got

home, she raced round the garden and then quietly went back to Sarah's side. Within days, she learned to join in Sarah's lively social life. At first, Sarah wasn't sure how Hazel would cope with the loud noisy parties that she often goes to with friends. But not only does Hazel enjoy them (she seems particularly partial to Irish music), she is also a good introduction to new friends. 'Before Hazel, I would sometimes sit in my chair and feel a bit awkward. Now, lots of people stop to stroke her, which provides a good opportunity for chatting.'

Like any other young girl, Sarah is very fashion conscious and Hazel loves going shopping with her. She particularly enjoys going into the changing room with her mistress and nosing under the curtains to see what other people are trying on. No one has ever objected but there have been a few startled cries of surprise. Hazel is also protective of Sarah's disabled friends and is particularly gentle if someone else arrives in a wheelchair. She will pick things up for them and seems to understand that this new guest has his or her own special needs. 'It makes me feel really good when she does this and it also makes me proud of her.'

The pair go on holiday together; Sarah is particularly keen on activity courses for the disabled. During a recent abseiling holiday, Hazel stayed at the bottom of the cliff, looking worriedly up, saying 'Can't you take me too?' She was, however, allowed on a sailing boat and loved sunbathing on the deck. Although Sarah had made herself have the confidence to go on holiday before Hazel, the dog has given her an extra boost. 'People are always commenting on her. And I know that if I got into trouble, she would bark and alert someone.'

Recently, Sarah has started a part-time administrative job; she sometimes takes Hazel along but if she doesn't, she's assured of a rapturous welcome when she gets home at the end of the day.

Back at home, Hazel is prepared to tackle almost anything, including the dizzy heights of the London Eye. During a recent trip, Hazel sat, mesmerised, at the lights below. 'Some of the other tourists were a bit worried that she might get